Pat Flynn

Flynnspired
Productions

DEAREST READER,

I'm trying to imagine all of the little moments that had to happen for you to arrive here today, reading the words that I've written for you in this letter.

Life is interesting like that. After all that has happened in the past, here we are together in the present. However you got here, I first just want to say, thank you.

Wherever you are in your journey, I hope *Let Go* becomes an important part of your own story, just like the events that happened in this book became a part of mine.

Although we are different people, all of us—you, me, our friends, family, community—every single person in this world shares the same struggle, and it's not just the tug of war between where we are and where we want to go, but who we believe we should be versus who we were meant to be.

The book you're about to read is more than a book—it's a call to action. The giant words on the cover are there to remind you about the best way to experience life's most amazing things.

Just *let go*.

It's not going to be easy, but just remember this: you're never going to be alone, either.

I'm looking forward to sharing my story with you, and I hope one day you'll share your story with me.

To the future!

FOR MY WIFE, APRIL, MY SON, KEONI, AND MY DAUGHTER, KAILANI.

CONTENTS

PART 2
LETTING GO, BY CHOICE

PREFACE
THE STORY OF THE ELEPHANT

Personal growth is hard. It's hard because taking risks is uncomfortable.

Such discomfort takes many devious forms: the fear of the unknown, the threat of ridicule, the possibility of disappointment. The thing is, we manufacture this stress ourselves. As Seth Godin says, "Anxiety is nothing but repeatedly re-experiencing failure in advance."

To unshackle ourselves from the limitations we allow ourselves to fall victim to, we must embrace a risky idea: letting go.

Like the adult elephant that was cruelly raised, tied to a small stake and short chain, many of us fail to realize our full potential because we don't let go of outdated beliefs and false realities. For the elephant, the reality is that he can easily break free of the stake and chain. But sadly, he's been conditioned to believe otherwise.

It's hard to think about the cruelty done to these magnificent animals. And thankfully, many people these days are fighting to change these awful practices. But in many places it's still common to secure a baby elephant to a stake and chain that, when he is small, can restrain him. Despite his natural instincts to break free and pursue his own path, he can't. After consistent exposure to this agony, he learns to accept the limitations as a permanent truth. Unfortunately, as he grows into a mighty adult, he never challenges what he has learned out of the belief that the effort will be futile, even painful.

Many of us suffer a similar experience. If we are to avoid a similar fate, we must first unlearn much of what conventional wisdom has taught us. Then, we are free to seize our potential.

I know how hard this path can be. I also know how rewarding it is. I came face to face with the risky idea of letting go in 2008. It was a scary time for my fiancée and me. But by believing and investing in myself, I was able to build the life of my dreams. *Let Go* is my chronicle of this journey. I hope you enjoy it. And more importantly, I hope you use it as a small force to break free and pursue your own path.

INTRODUCTION

In late 2012, I got a long email from a man in Poland named Michal Szafranski. In the email, Michal told me about a drastic life change he'd recently gone through.

He had broken both of his legs in a snowboarding accident several years earlier, followed by a long and intense period of rehab and recovery. Four years later, he was struggling to get back to where he was before his injury and feeling defeated.

Michal's accident had been devastating—a bad landing following a jump off a snowboard ramp had caused both of his legs to shatter. Before the accident, Michal had been a working man, but the accident had prevented him from returning to work. He had fallen into a state of depression, especially because he felt he could no longer support his family.

As he was on his bed recovering one day in early 2012, Michal decided to find some podcasts to fill his time, and that's when he discovered my podcast, the *Smart Passive Income (SPI)* podcast. On the podcast, I talk a lot about goal setting, and one of the things I always mention when I discuss setting goals is that you have to reach high—to set almost impossible goals for yourself. Even if at the time it seems like something you won't be able to achieve, set that goal for yourself anyway.

So, after listening to an episode in which I shared this exact advice, Michal decided to set himself an impossible-seeming goal to help jump-start things: He was going to run a marathon later that year. Around the same time, Michal had also decided to start a blog to share personal finance tips. He continued to listen to the *SPI* podcast, and to read the *SPI* blog, for resources and inspiration as he built his blog and started writing content.

He was making great progress, but he also started to realize that the marathon he'd committed to was approaching more quickly than he'd realized. With only months to get into shape, Michal was feeling unprepared and overwhelmed, wondering if the goal he'd set was just a bit too audacious. Here's what Michal told me about that time:

Do you remember what I have been telling my friends since April? I've been telling everyone that I will run a marathon this September. As the end of May was coming, I still hadn't started my training. I realized it was very late. I started looking for excuses. I even started thinking how I would explain to everyone why I'm not going to complete the marathon this year due to a lot of work, etc. I already felt like a loser... and I hated the feeling. Then I started listening to your podcasts. Your positive energy and motivating message of "work hard now and reap benefits later" has completely changed my mind.

Michal told me how listening to my podcasts helped renew his excitement and his commitment to run the grueling race. But after a little while, he realized his training time was cutting into his podcast-listening time. So, he came up with a novel solution—he brought me on as his virtual trainer by listening to my podcasts in his head-phones during his training runs in order to, as he put it, "optimize" his listening:

Listening to you, Pat, during my 660 km of training was a great experience. Sometimes I laughed, sometimes I cried during my run. I remember many stories from your podcasts. One was the story of an ill man who was listening to your podcasts again and again. I was doing the same. You've become a very good, close friend to me. Strange but true.

Fast-forward to September 2012. Michal sent me a long email, telling me how he had finished the Warsaw Marathon in four hours and twenty-three minutes. At the bottom of the email was a picture of Michal crossing the finish line, holding a banner that he'd kept stuffed in his pocket the entire race. The banner read, in Polish:

Thank you God—and you Gabi, Szym, Ida [Michal's wife and kids], parents, DCS [Michal's company] & Pat Flynn.

Michal told me that after enlisting me as his headphone trainer, he'd decided to do two things:

1) Follow as many of your suggestions as I can, and be as generous and helpful to others as I can.

2) Do something for you, Pat, as a small gift for all the good things you've done for me.

Michal's small gift was including me in his dedication when he crossed the finish line and conquered the Warsaw Marathon. Needless to say, to me, this gift felt like more than enough.

· · · · ·

READING MICHAL'S STORY was an incredibly moving experience— to be honest, I was a mess, tears pouring down my face and onto my keyboard as I read it. But it was also incredibly motivating. His email had reached me during a low point in my own life, when I was considering giving up on my podcast. He helped me realize that there's more to the work I do than just thank yous, blog comments, and passive income. He showed me that there are people on the other end whose lives could be changed by what I was doing—and basically saved my podcast in the process. He showed me that I had to keep going, because sometimes you don't truly know the impact you're having on someone else.

By the way, Michal is now something of a celebrity in Poland. His blog, jakoszczedzacpieniadze.pl, is now one of the top finance blogs in the country. He's self-published a number one best-selling book, *Finansowy ninja* [Finance ninja], and has been featured in the Polish mainstream media a number of times. You can read Michal's email to me and learn more about his incredible story in my October 2012 Income Report (smartpassiveincome.com/income-reports/my-october-2012-monthly-income-report).

I wrote the first edition of the book you're holding in your hands (or reading on your screen) in 2013. Since then, I've heard from many people who have told me how I've helped them achieve goals and overcome hurdles in their lives and their businesses. Not all of those stories have been as monumental as Michal's——that would be a tall order. But if there's one thing I've learned over the past nine years, it's this: the more I make my business about serving and helping others, the more meaningful my work becomes, and the greater the impact I can have.

A lot of people see my success and say, "Pat has everything. Pat is special. Pat is not like me." But none of those things are true. Although "on paper" it might seem like I'm very successful and have everything together, I definitely don't! I'm always learning. I'm always stumbling. I'm always growing. And, perhaps the biggest one: as I continue to grow, in life and in business, I'm always meeting new challenges and limiting beliefs, and I have to learn to let go of those, too. I believe the universe tests us every time we try to do something important, just to make sure we're the right ones to do it. Since the publication of the first edition of this book in 2013, the universe has thrown a lot of tests my way, and I've had to let go of dozens of beliefs that have held me back.

As Ramit Sethi, author of *I Will Teach You To Be Rich*, once told me in a pivotal conversation (more on that in "The Madness"), "What got you here, won't get you there." You can choose to stay where you are

if it's working for you, but if you want to get to the next level, you're going to have to be willing to make some changes. You're going to have to critically examine all of your beliefs and your practices, and let go of the ones that are holding you back. That may be the biggest thing I've learned so far in my journey, and it's what this book is about.

•   •   •   •   •

SO WHY A SPECIAL edition of *Let Go* to commemorate the 10-year anniversary of my layoff, and not just a brand new book? I thought you might ask.

The first edition of *Let Go* was my first true passion project outside of online business. I wrote the book because a lot of people had been asking me to tell my story—to give them a better sense of who I was, where I came from, and how I'd built my business to that point.

That first edition was transformational for a lot of people. I talked to teachers and professors who shared it with their students to help them understand what might be ahead in their lives after they graduated. I heard from church groups who used the book to build entire weekend programs around the idea of letting go. It's been a true blessing to see people benefit from my story.

Because of this, there's a special place in my heart for the first edition of *Let Go*. But more than that, in seeing the impact of the book I understood that even though *Let Go* was about my story, it was no longer just about me. So much more has happened since the book was finished, and I've learned so much. I wanted to find a way to continue my story, to reach and serve more people with more substance and guidance—and creating an anniversary edition of *Let Go* seemed like a perfect way to do just that.

I also realized that I didn't have to come up with a whole new book concept to continue my story. The trigger moment for this realization came on the heels of the success of a good friend. In 2017, my friend S.J. Scott released a second edition of his book *Habit Stacking*, and that edition quickly went on to become a *Wall Street Journal* best seller. I was really surprised when I found this out. How does a second edition of a self-published book become a *Wall Street Journal* bestseller?

Then I said, "Why not *Let Go*?" Seeing Steve publish a second edition and get his book into even more hands inspired me. It made me realize that you don't have to start from scratch to put something out there that can make a difference to people. You can build on what you've done before, adding even more value to what you delivered the first time around.

•   •   •   •   •

THIS 10-YEAR ANNIVERSARY Edition of *Let Go* was designed with one main purpose: to give you a view into your potential future. I want you to not only feel inspired about what's possible, but also to understand some of the struggles and challenges that might be coming your way as you build your business and create the life you want to live. I want you to learn from my lessons so you can apply them when you meet similar challenges on your own path. I want you to walk away from this book a little more prepared for what's to come.

I was on somebody else's path for a long time, and it wasn't until I got laid off that I finally became conscious of the fact that I could choose my own path. I promise you that if you become conscious of what's holding you back, you can do the same—no layoff necessary.

So who exactly is this book for? It's for people who need a guide, someone who's maybe just a few steps ahead of them and can show them what might lie ahead. It's for people who feel like they're running out of inspiration or options and need somebody they can trust. And it's for people who may not realize that they need to make letting go part of their DNA if they want to evolve and improve, who need to know that it's okay, and important, to let go of some things in order to grow.

It's hard to see the future, and it can be tricky to let go of something that's holding you back, especially if you don't even know it's there. With this 10-Year Anniversary Edition, I want to give you a sense of the things you might need to let go of in your own journey, so you can anticipate and prepare for them—so you won't be surprised by the challenges that pop up and can instead take action from them.

I also want to open your eyes to the fact that success doesn't come easily. It's not an A to Z kind of thing, but a zigzag process, one with a lot of moments that'll make you want to give up. As a result, I know how important it is to have someone in your corner who can lead you by example. I want to help you understand that you're not alone, and that even the most successful people go through deep struggles.

Who is this book *not* for? It's not for the people who feel like they have all the answers. If that describes you, great! You already have some things figured out—and that's awesome.

Ultimately, I want to help you see not just what I've been through, but what you can learn and take away from my journey. While this second edition is not exactly a manual or how-to, a "do this, then that" kind of guide to success in online entrepreneurship, it will hopefully serve as a beacon for you. I hope that by sharing with you the lessons I've learned over the past nine years, you can use them to light your own path.

· · · · ·

THE TITLE OF the original book, *Let Go*, was mostly about being let go from my job in 2009—but it was also about having to let go of the path I was *told* I should be on, one that was very hard for me to leave. I had spent my whole life trying to get perfect grades, get into a great

I WANT **YOU** TO WALK AWAY FROM THIS BOOK A LITTLE MORE **PREPARED** FOR WHAT'S TO COME.

college, and then climb the corporate ladder, only to have that ladder swept out from under me.

Since then, "letting go" has become even more to me. And so *Let Go* is a call to action. It's a rallying cry for those who feel stuck and don't know what to do next.

In a word, letting go is about *courage*. Courage is a really cool word, because it has two parts. There's the letting go part—letting go of the fear, the limiting beliefs. Courage to make the decision to break free from the things that are holding you back. But courage is not just about letting go. It's also about climbing higher, and reaching for something new.

When my son, Keoni, was younger, he was afraid of ladders. We were at Disneyland once, and our room had a bunk bed. Keoni really wanted to climb up to the top bunk, but as soon as he stepped onto the first rung of the ladder and found himself off the ground a little bit, he froze. Even though he was only a foot off the ground and he could have easily caught himself if he had fallen, being in this position put him in a state of fear.

The way he started to get over this fear was to understand that he could ascend the ladder by taking just one arm or a leg off at a time. He could let go a little bit and still be safe. When he started to think of it that way, letting go a little bit at a time, he saw that climbing the ladder wasn't an all-or-nothing process: he wasn't going to jump right up to the top, and he wasn't going to come crashing down either. He always had three limbs supporting him, keeping him safe, while the fourth limb helped him climb higher.

Seeing my son grapple with the bunk ladder, I was struck by the simple power of letting go of what you need to while holding on to the things that support you. It still takes effort, coordination, and strength to climb this way. But once you've let go and reached for the next rung, you can do it again and keep going higher.

By the end of this book, I want you to be conscious about what's holding you back, to see more clearly the beliefs that are keeping you from letting go and grabbing hold of that next rung on the ladder. Then, I want you to find the courage to let go of those beliefs so you can move forward and upward. This process will be scary, but that's okay. After all, there are great things waiting for you at the top of the ladder—and even at the next rung.

· · · · ·

FINALLY, A QUICK note about how this book is structured. Although the first edition of *Let Go* was timeline driven, the updated material in this second edition is less chronological. Instead, it's structured around a few main topics that cover the biggest themes in my journey—from establishing the mindset necessary for success, to the madness of entrepreneurship, to the mechanics of what my business looks like and how it has evolved. (Yep, there are a lot of *M*s in this book.)

If you've already read the first edition of *Let Go*, the 10-Year Anniversary Edition picks up where the first one left off. If you haven't read the first edition—or you have but it's been a while—start at the beginning. And even if you've heard my story, or parts of it, somewhere else (on stage, in a podcast episode, in a blog post)—the first part is a great place to learn the details of where I came from and how I started my journey.

After all, even though we always have to "let go" of our past in a way, it's still important to remember where we came from, so we can appreciate the journey and understand just how much we've achieved and overcome.

LET-TING GO, BY CIRCUM-STANCE

NOVEMBER

2005

"Luck is being in the right place at the right time but location and timing are to some extent under our control."

Natasha Josefowitz

PETE HAD ASKED EVERYONE AROUND THE TABLE, AND THEN IT WAS MY TURN.

"And how about you, Pat? What are you majoring in?"

"Architecture," I replied.

"Oh, really? What kind of architecture do you want to get into? Commercial? Residential?"

"Actually, I was thinking about getting into restaurant design."

Pete nodded his head slowly on a tilt, "Interesting . . ."

Pete Osborne was the owner of the very restaurant we were all having dinner in that evening: Momo's, located right outside of SBC Park (now known as AT&T Park) in San Francisco. Being a University of California Berkeley alum and a former sousaphone player in the marching band, he liked to invite the executive committee of the band to his restaurant each year to meet the new faces and stay in touch.

Pete looked at me with a smile that ran from ear to ear.

"I'll tell you what, Pat; I'm going to give my buddy John McNulty a call for you tomorrow. He's a principal at MBH Architects in Alameda and a fellow Cal alum. He helped design Momo's, in fact. I'll tell him to give you a call."

I immediately found out how difficult it is to say thank you when your mouth is wide open (try it), but something auditory must have come out of my voice box, because afterward I heard him say, "My pleasure, Pat."

Pete glanced back at the kitchen. "Please excuse me for a second. They need me back of house for something. I'll be right back."

After Pete exited, my equally wide-eyed companions all leaned in toward the center of the table and discreetly congratulated me. Will, the drum major who was sitting to my left, gave me a congratulatory tap with his fist on my shoulder: about a four out of ten on the hurt scale.

I was stoked about what had just happened, but I didn't want to get too excited about it yet. Yes, I had been looking for a job at an architecture firm for a few months at that point, to no avail. That's precisely why I wasn't expecting anything. I wasn't even attending this event to look for a job; I was there to represent the band and enjoy an amazing dinner that was not from the dining commons.

Plus, people make promises all the time, but only a percentage of them actually follow through. So I told myself, "If I get a call, great. If not, I won't get too upset."

About a four out of ten on the hurt scale.

My skepticism aside, the rest of the evening was amazing. Many more stories were told and laughs were had when Pete came back to the table. I ended up having such a great time that I totally forgot about Pete's offer.

Dinner had never tasted so good.

· · · · ·

THE NEXT DAY at around three in the afternoon, I received a call from John McNulty, principal at MBH Architects. The day after that, I went in for an interview and was hired on the spot as an entry-level drafter in the restaurant division of the firm.

Mind blown.

Everything was finally paying off: all of the studying, the homework, the good grades, and excessive extracurriculars on my record that were there just to impress admissions.

It's incredible how things work out sometimes, especially when you least expect them to. Sure, I was in the right place at the right time, but every decision I made before that call—from choosing to go to Cal to joining the marching band to running for Student Director and even going to dinner that night—was a decision I made on my own that put me in front of those opportunities.

It wasn't luck; it was reward.

And so the path continued.

FEBRU ARY
MARCH
2006

The path to success is to take massive, determined action.

Tony Robbins

IN **ARCHITECTURE** SCHOOL, I USED TO PUT A DIGITAL CAMERA INSIDE THE MODELS THAT I BUILT TO PHOTOGRAPH THE INTERIORS.

Later, I used Photoshop to add people walking

around in the pictures. At the time, it was my life goal

to make those conceptual visions a reality. The idea

that I could design something that people could

experience and remember obsessed me.

When I started working at MBH Architects I tried to make design suggestions like I did back in school. Unfortunately, I quickly realized that as an entry-level drafter I had absolutely no say on anything related to design. My job was to make sure someone else's designs were properly entered into AutoCAD, period.

My limited on-paper responsibilities didn't blunt my determination to show my higher-ups that I was meant to be much more than a drafter. So, I worked hard. I read books, took classes, and did pretty much everything else that wasn't asked of me or listed in my job description.

Sixty to seventy hours a week was normal; eighty to one hundred was commonplace when there was a deadline. I loved every minute of it. I must have made an impression because after a year I was promoted ... to senior drafter.

I was still a drafter; I was just . . . senior, I guess.

The paycheck I earned every fifteen days finally crept above $1,000, but I was still staring lifelessly at my computer all day. I could feel my eyes going bad and posture getting stressed. And I continued to have no influence on design. Worse, I was now the guy who people could blame if something in the drawings was wrong.

Looking up at the ladder, Job Captain was the next rung on the climb to the top. Promoting anyone with less than four or five years' experience to Job Captain was unheard of, especially when that someone had little to no experience in the field. I wasn't going to let that stop me from trying, though, so I decided to add more to my plate.

Typically, someone in my position would start the slow and long haul toward an architecture license, which, at least in California, requires a minimum eight years of post-secondary education or work experience, completion of the Internship Development program, passing the Architecture Registration Examination (which is made up of seven different tests), and an oral exam.

Instead of following this path to licensure like all of the other young professionals in the office, I decided to look for a different path, one where I could more quickly add to my list of architecture-related accomplishments as well as stand out from the crowd.

Again, I did anything I could to impress. So, I started studying to become a LEED© Accredited Professional (AP).

LEED, short for Leadership in Energy and Environmental Design, was a relatively new and trending standard related to designing projects that quantifiably make less of an impact on the environment. This standard was surging in the world of architecture because everything was "going green" at the time.

A LEED AP is a person who is capable of overseeing and managing the LEED certification process for a new or existing building. To become a LEED AP, all you need to do is pass an exam that demonstrates your

I DECIDED TO LOOK FOR A DIFFERENT PATH

knowledge of LEED principles, practices, and procedures. Unfortunately, the exam had a passing rate below 35 percent. This was not going to be easy.

When I first started studying for the exam, I took to paper and pen like I did back in college. I quickly discovered that getting back into "study mode" was extremely difficult since this time I had no lesson plan, homework, or professors to guide me. It had been a couple of years since I last had to memorize material for an exam, and my brain just wasn't having it. After a couple of weeks, I gave up.

A month and a move later (to our sister office in Irvine), I decided to give the LEED AP exam another shot, but this time I took a completely different approach: I studied by creating a blog to hold and organize my notes.

InTheLEED.com. I thought it was pretty clever. (Later, I found out that using a trademark in a domain name isn't really a good idea. I later changed the website to GreenExamAcademy.com. Lesson learned.)

I knew the blog would help in several different ways:

First, the blog would allow me to access and search my notes from anywhere I had Internet connectivity. I traveled a lot, so this was very helpful. My laptop replaced my messy bundle of notebooks.

Second, the exam material referenced a lot of websites, so I could include those specific links on my blog, which would make studying much easier.

Third, the blog just organized everything much better. By categorizing and tagging my notes, I could easily see how things related to each other. Consequently, I started to really understand the material better than if I'd only had reams of paper notes.

Most importantly, I envisioned the blog as something "tangible" that I could show the higher-ups in the firm. By taking the lead and building a resource that anyone else in the office could study from, I figured my superiors would recognize my abilities as ahead of the rest.

So every day I added more notes and uploaded more pictures, charts, and graphs onto the blog—anything that would help me remember what I needed to know to pass the exam.

On March 8, 2008, after six months of studying hardcore for two to three hours a day, I passed the exam and became a LEED Accredited Professional, one of the few LEED APs in the entire firm. A month later, I was promoted to Job Captain, one of the youngest people in the firm to ever become one. My salary nearly doubled to $60,000 per year. I couldn't have been more pumped.

On March 31, 2008, I proposed to my girlfriend, April. She said yes. Life was good.

And so the path continued.

MAY 2008 JUNE

"Everyone has a plan 'til they get punched in the mouth."

Mike Tyson

A NEW TITLE, NEW BUSINESS CARDS, AND NEW RESPONSI-BILITIES.

I was exactly where I wanted to be and sort of felt like I had time-traveled to get there; everything had happened so fast. Unfortunately, I think my quick acceleration disrupted the space-time continuum, because a couple of months later things started to go bad.

Really bad.

With the slowing US economy and many companies starting to focus on survival instead of expansion, the architecture industry took a huge hit. Nobody was building anything, so nobody needed architects.

Firms throughout the nation began cutting staff in droves. Even world-famous firms like Gehry Partners and Gensler were laying off people by the truckload just to stay afloat. For a lesser-known company like ours, the outlook was not good.

By May, over a hundred people in our firm were no longer employed. We called it getting "slayed off" because it was more than just losing a job; it felt like murder. I'd come into the office the next day and find more desks clear of objects and more seats clear of occupants. I still remember what it was like seeing them there. Even people who had been working for the firm for over a decade were being laid off.

"What was going to happen to them? Their families? Their career? What was going to happen to me?" I wondered.

One by one, people in our office were called into a meeting with the principal and returned a totally different person. I felt like I was in a sick reality TV show where people were getting voted off the island. I couldn't help but wonder if I was next.

All of a sudden, my turn came to have a chat with my boss.

I stayed positive. I had survived this long; maybe he was calling me in to tell me not to worry. Maybe it was just a pay cut. I'd be okay with a pay cut at that point. Maybe it was just temporary until things got back on track. I had just been promoted; they couldn't possibly lay me off for good, right?

I crept into my boss's office.

"Have a seat, Pat," he said.

I sat down, but I didn't say a word. I was just there to hear the verdict. Nothing I could say or do now would change it.

"Pat, you're one of the youngest, brightest minds we have in this entire firm . . ."

A glimpse of hope.

"But unfortunately . . ."

Never mind.

"As you know, things have been rough, and we've tried to keep you as long as possible. At this point, we have no choice but to let you go. I'm sorry."

Me too.

JUNE 2008

"My fault, my failure, is not in the passions I have, but in my lack of control of them.

Jack Kerouac

"WE HAVE TO LET YOU GO. I'M SORRY."

Upon hearing those words, something the size of a golf ball materialized deep in my throat. I started chewing the back of my tongue to try and make the feeling go away.

None of this made sense to me. None of it. I had done everything right, everything that I was supposed to do, and this was the outcome?

I wondered, "What am I going to tell April? Will we have to put our wedding on hold? What am I going to do for work? How am I going to pay rent? Will my parents be disappointed in me? Is this all my fault?"

Luckily (sort of) my boss told me that I was in charge of a few projects that still needed my personal attention, so they couldn't let me go right away. I was told I had until the later half of October before I was gone for good, which meant I had a few months to figure things out. I appreciated the heads up, but it didn't soften the blow.

My first move was to try to get a job at another architecture firm. I was a Job Captain willing to take an entry-level position if I had to, anything just to survive. As soon as I got back to my desk, I spent an hour calling fifteen different firms to see if there were any positions available.

Nothing.

Next, I called almost every construction and engineering firm that our company had worked with in the past.

Again, nothing.

The reality of the situation was that I wasn't going to get another job in this industry any time soon.

· · · · ·

I LEFT WORK an hour early to go home and think about what I would say to April. She usually came over after work for dinner. I wasn't really hungry, though, thanks to the golf ball still lodged in my throat.

April called me around six p.m., which meant she was at the door to my apartment. She could tell that something was wrong the moment I opened the door, even before the tears started to crawl down my face a few seconds later.

"What's wrong?! What happened?!" she asked.

I didn't answer.

"Are you okay?"

After a few seconds of silence, I shrugged my shoulders.

"What happened?" she asked again.

"I don't have a job anymore. I was laid off."

More tears started to blur my vision, but I looked at April's face to see her reaction, and her eyes started to well up too.

"It's okay," she said. "It's okay. We'll figure something out."

Another few seconds of silence passed.

"I'm sorry."

And then April replied with the most perfect words in the world, "Stop it. This isn't your fault. We're going to be okay."

That was exactly what I needed to hear. It wasn't my fault; stuff just happens sometimes. No matter what, we were going to be okay; we would just have to play with the cards that had been dealt to us. We were going to be okay.

WE WOULD JUST HAVE TO PLAY WITH THE CARDS THAT HAD BEEN DEALT TO US.

WITH ABOUT THREE months left before I would officially be let go, April and I decided it would make sense for both of us to move back in with our parents. We'd go from paying two separate rent checks, to none. Plus food, laundry, and other mini-perks that come with living at home with the 'rents, although that's not really where we wanted to be. No offense, Mom and Dad.

Unfortunately for me, our parents lived in San Diego, eighty miles south of my temporary position in Irvine. Telecommuting was not an option, so I was looking at an hour and a half commute each way. With gas prices at an all-time high (nearly $5 per gallon in some areas of Southern California), taking the train instead made more economical sense. Two hours to work in the morning, and then two hours back at night.

At least I didn't have to fight traffic.

TAKING THE TRAIN was not as bad as I thought it would be. Sure, I'd wake up at four a.m. to get ready in time for a five thirty departure, but the train hugged the shoreline during the entire commute. I admired the hardcore surfers who were up early to catch the day's first set of waves. Later, I'd catch the silhouettes of them in the evening on my way home as the sun set behind them. The scene was like moving art, every single day.

Although I was still going to work each day (if you could call it work), the inevitable was creeping up on me and my mind had already checked out. I looked forward to the train rides more than I did actually arriving at their destination.

Since I had a lot of time on my hands during my daily commute, I began to make use of it. At first, I listened to music on my iPod, but it often put me to sleep and I was worried that I might miss a stop.

That's when I started to make a habit of listening to podcasts instead. In my quest to find great shows to fill up my iPod, I stumbled upon one in particular that I quickly became addicted to: *Internet Business Mastery* (IBM), hosted by Jeremy and Jay. The show was about how to build a business online. They often shared the success stories and tips from those who had done so already. It was inspiring and educational, which made me think, a lot. It made me think about choosing my own path, creating my own freedom, and possibly working for myself instead.

But what about the path that I was supposed to be on? Maybe that didn't matter. Maybe it was time for a new direction. Maybe I was meant for a different path.

"Man can learn nothing except by going from the known to the unknown."

Claude Bernard

I DIDN'T KNOW ANYTHING ABOUT HOW TO START A BUSINESS, LET ALONE ONE THAT WAS ONLINE.

My only experience with making any sort of money online was from selling Magic: The Gathering cards on eBay. This whole "make a living online" thing always seemed a little shady to me, but the *IBM* podcast was showing me a different light.

Besides the motivating commentary by hosts Jeremy and Jay and the incredible number of tips that didn't make sense to me at the time, the podcast occasionally featured success stories from their community of listeners.

In episode thirty-six, I was introduced to Shaun Noonan. Shaun and his wife, Cici, made a fantastic living by teaching others how to speak Indonesian through their website. In another episode, I learned about Cornelius Fichtner, who found his freedom by teaching others how to become a project manager and pass an exam.

And that's when the light bulb turned on.

I already had a website about passing the LEED exam. It had just been sitting untouched for several months. Maybe I could fine-tune it for others and somehow turn it into a business.

"But where do I start?"

I didn't know exactly what to do next, but I did have a lot of questions:

"Will people even use my website? How will they find it? Is this even legal? How will it make money? What if this fails?"

Then a remarkable thought appeared:

"What if . . . this works?"

The anxiety kicked in, but in a good way. I was pumped! I had nothing to lose, so I started to read more about online business. I printed articles that I'd found online and purchased a few books to take with me on the train. The train ride was no longer about scenic views over the ocean anymore; it was my classroom.

One of the first things I learned was that a website does no good unless there's traffic coming to it, so naturally I added a stat-tracking tool to the website so that I could keep tabs on the number of people who visited.

The next day, I woke up to an unbelievable surprise. At 4:45 in the morning I checked my stats and it showed me that 5,158 people had visited my site the day before.

That couldn't be right. No way. I quadruple-checked. I thought maybe that was how many times I had visited the site on my own prior to that day when I was studying, but all of those hits registered the day before, and from over fifty countries around the world. My site was already serving those looking to pass the LEED exam, and I didn't even know it!

After the initial shock, heavy breathing, and checking the stats again just to make sure, I dug deeper to see where all that traffic was coming from. I had never mentioned my website to anyone except the people in my office. I thought maybe no more than twenty people knew about it, two hundred if it was the entire firm, but that was highly unlikely.

When I clicked on "traffic sources" I saw that 81 percent of my traffic was coming directly from Google search. I immediately launched Google in my web browser, typed in "leed exam," and hit enter. There I was, second position from the top. I typed in "leed ap exam" and hit enter. There I was again, second position from the top. Every single keyword that I typed in that I thought people who wanted to take the LEED AP exam would use summoned my website. People were finding it on their own!

I also had a good number of visitors coming from various websites that linked to my site. A few of them were actually chapter websites for the United States Green Building Council (USGBC), the organization that actually administers the LEED exam.

I couldn't believe it. Here I was sitting on a website that had thousands of visitors a day and I didn't even know it. How long this had been going on, I'll never know.

My next step was to make sure that the site was user-friendly. I created a little "about" page that described who I was and why I had originally created the site. I added articles about what the exam process was like and what to expect. Then, I enabled the ability to leave comments on my posts. Within five minutes of doing that, my first comment arrived. The commenter asked for clarification about something on the exam that I happened to know the answer to, so I responded. More comments started coming in day after day. It was hard to believe, but a community was forming right before my eyes. Knowing that I was genuinely helping people, and that they appreciated that help, was an amazing feeling.

My next task was to figure out if I could actually make money from the site. I searched Google and at first the only thing that came up were scammy-looking websites that were asking me to pay for "the secrets to becoming a millionaire." I didn't want to become a millionaire; I just wanted to know if making money online was possible.

Finally, I came across an article on ProBlogger.net written in 2004 about Google AdSense, a program you can sign up for that provides a simple code you insert into your website that automatically generates ads relevant to the content on your website. You'll earn a little money if anyone clicks on those ads.

I signed up for AdSense and had one ad showing on the homepage of my website after just a half hour. Thirty minutes later, I logged into my account and saw I had earned $1.08!

My first dollar online, and the best feeling in the world.

AUGUST

28

2002

"I am still learning."

Michelangelo

I COULD EASILY FIND MORE CHANGE ON THE FLOOR OF MY TRUCK,

but the $1.08 that I earned on my website made

me realize that this could really happen. It was

almost like that dollar appeared out of nowhere.

Of course, that was far from the truth. I had put a lot of hours into the site prior to my first dollar. If you were to calculate an hourly wage based on those earnings, it would be a fraction of a penny per hour. Nonetheless, I was more motivated than ever.

I became obsessed with checking my stats. Every ten minutes I would log back into my account to see if I had earned more money. When I did, I would do a little fist pump and smile. When the total didn't change, I'd start to worry that maybe my website was down. It's funny how insane this was making me; it was like nothing I had ever experienced before. After that first day of running ads, I had earned just a little over $5.00.

The next day at work, I continued to refresh my AdSense account every few minutes. There wasn't much work to do, but I'd still hide my browser window every time someone walked by. Now that I think about it, what were they going to do, fire me?

After a few days monitoring my Google AdSense revenue, $10 to $15 a day seemed to be average, which was fantastic but definitely not enough to live off of. I was getting married in a few months. As much as I'd like to say that I would have been okay if April was the one doing the breadwinning, as a man and a husband I knew I would feel like I wasn't doing my part.

I decided to take some of my earnings and invest in an online course for building a successful online business. Jeremy and Jay, the hosts of the *Internet Business Mastery* podcast, came out with the IBM Academy: a membership site with training materials and a forum with other like-minded people who were all doing business online.

The lessons in the Academy were very helpful. I already had a website so I skipped a few lessons here and there, but I was able to tweak a number of things and increase my AdSense earnings to about $30 per day almost immediately. There weren't any specific tips for AdSense, but the strategies I learned for getting more traffic to my site and keeping people on my site longer probably helped with my earnings.

The best part about the Academy was the forum. There were a couple hundred members who all had different stories to share and reasons for being there, but the drive to succeed was all the same.

It was infectious.

Region-specific groups existed within the forum so that people could connect locally if they wanted. There was a group for people who lived in Southern California, and I became friends with all of them. We would check in virtually with each other every so often, which was nice to have. I didn't know anybody else who was into what I was doing online, so it was nice to be able to chat about it.

•   •   •   •   •

A COUPLE WEEKS after I joined the Academy, Jeremy announced that he was moving to San Diego. When our little SoCal group heard about this, we immediately reached out to him and decided to all meet in person once he arrived.

It was a random Thursday afternoon near the end of July 2008. I had gotten the day off from work as well as the next. We all planned to meet at a Panera Bread that was just about five minutes from my parents' home. I didn't really know what to expect from the meeting. The only thing I knew was that I was going to order a half sandwich and soup for dinner.

After I parked my truck I saw a group of people sitting outside the restaurant. I immediately recognized Jeremy and some of the other faces from the forum, but there were a few people I didn't recognize either. I felt like a fish out of water. I was already starting to sweat at the idea that I'd actually have to talk in front of everybody.

I walked up to the group and quickly introduced myself. Everybody was very friendly. Hands were shaken all around. I relaxed a little.

We started the meeting by going around the circle one by one and introducing ourselves and what we were doing online. We all seemed to be at various stages, but the others were obviously earning a lot more than I was. Nobody was using AdSense, and a lot of the things they talked about I didn't even understand. Then it was my turn.

"Hi. My name is Pat. I work at an architecture firm in Irvine, but I'm being let go in a couple of months. I started a website that helps people pass an exam in the architecture industry and I make a few dollars a day with Google AdSense."

It was a much shorter introduction than the others', but I didn't know what else to say. I wasn't even sure if I belonged, and I didn't want to waste anyone's time. Then someone followed up with, "How much traffic do you get to your site?"

"It depends," I replied. "Sometimes six or seven thousand visits."

"A month?"

"A day."

They all looked stunned.

Then Jeremy, with eyes wide open, said, "Pat! You have to write and sell an ebook on your site!"

Everyone else agreed with excitement. I wanted to be excited too, but the only thing I could think was, "What's an ebook?"

I WANTED TO BE EXCITED TOO, BUT THE ONLY THING THAT I COULD THINK WAS, "WHAT'S AN EBOOK?"

AUGUST
UST
SEPT
2008
EMBER
BER

"Faith and doubt are both needed—not as antagonists, but working side by side to take us around the unknown curve."

Lillian Smith

AN EBOOK. THAT'S WHAT I NEEDED TO MAKE, BUT WHAT WAS IT EXACTLY? I DIDN'T KNOW FOR SURE.

I was embarrassed to ask the group directly so I asked a question that didn't make me sound quite as lost as I really was.

"How would you do it?"

The ensuing conversation was the best education I'd had in years. My right hand cramped trying to write down all the great advice everyone was sharing.

I learned that an ebook was simply an electronic book that people could download and read on their computers. I could create it in Microsoft Word, export it as a PDF, and sell it for a price on my website.

The process made sense on the surface and seemed doable, but one thing in particular worried me as soon as I started to get excited about the whole idea: What would I put in the book? Everything that anyone needed to pass the LEED exam was already freely available on my website. Why would anyone pay for the same information when they could already get it for free?

I expressed my concern to the group.

"Don't worry about it," one person explained. "People will pay if it does the job. If it provides any sort of value, people will pay for it."

Another person added, "An ebook is more convenient. It may be the same information that you have on your website, but it'll be packaged and more convenient for people to read. People pay for convenience. Not everyone wants to study from a website."

One other person put it bluntly when he said, "What have you got to lose?"

Nothing.

I returned home from the meeting positively stoked. I couldn't go to sleep that night because I was too busy writing the outline for my ebook. I didn't know how I was going to sell it, what it was going to look like, or even what the title would be. I just knew that I had to compile all of the text on my website into a neatly ordered document, so I started with that.

I could figure out how to sell it later.

·　·　·　·　·

EVERY NIGHT I would put in three to four hours of work on the ebook. I didn't go out with friends. I didn't watch TV. I didn't play video games. I just hustled on my book.

The process was fun at first. I kept imagining what it would be like to actually sell a book to someone. That energy pushed me forward. After a few weeks, however, I started to struggle. I thought I would be done, but formatting the ebook in Word so that it looked more like a workbook than a novel was proving to be quite difficult. Frustration and confusion began to mount. Soon after, I started to question whether or not creating an ebook was a good idea at all.

"Am I just wasting my time?"

One morning during breakfast, my dad started to confuse me even more. "You know, now is the perfect time to go back to school," he said. "You could get your master's degree, and by the time you finish school the job market might be up again."

My dad was right. He was always right. That's why I was confused. I couldn't get a job in architecture but I could definitely go back to school and still get ahead while the market was down. The initiative would definitely impress any potential employers. And I'd be able to start at a higher salary than I'd ended with.

That day, at the office while doing nothing, I thought long and hard about what my dad said. He was totally right, but going back to school didn't feel right for me. I'd worked my butt off since middle school to make sure I got the best grades. I'd joined clubs and volunteered several hours just so it would look good on my record. I'd followed the path exactly as outlined by society only to be kicked off. And here I was thinking about trying to get back on?

No.

No more.

Forget that.

It was time to let go of the path and carve out my own.

"If I fail, I want it to be because of my own faults, not because of something I couldn't control," I thought. "After all, what have I got to lose?"

Nothing, but the opportunity.

· · · · ·

I FINISHED WRITING the LEED ebook two weeks later. The book was 102 pages long. I knew it was the best resource for passing the LEED exam that had ever existed. I converted it to a PDF, saved it to my desktop, and sat back. There it was, sitting on my desktop: *The LEED AP Walkthrough*, by Pat Flynn.

"Now, how do I sell this thing?"

Luckily, I knew exactly where to go to figure that out without wasting any time.

SEPTEMBER 2008 OCTOBER

"Life begins at the end of your comfort zone."

Neale Donald Walsch

I HAD A FINISHED PRODUCT, BUT HAD NO IDEA HOW TO SELL IT.

Selling an ebook wasn't like advertising, where all I had to worry about was one single line of code on my website; selling a digital product was a whole different beast.

Instead of fumbling around trying to figure it out on my own, I went back to my group of friends online who had sold products before and asked them, "Where do I go from here?"

They gave me a number of different options, all of which seemed viable, but one in particular seemed to be perfect for my situation: E-junkie.com, an online digital delivery service. All you have to do is sign up, upload your digital product (in my case, a PDF) to E-junkie's server, and place the resulting product-specific code on your website. This code displays a "Buy Now" button that your visitors can click on. When clicked, the button starts the e-commerce checkout process. After payment, E-junkie will automatically send the customer an email that contains a link to download the product.

The system seemed like science fiction. I couldn't believe this kind of thing was possible. I could actually sell my ebook without having to process and deliver each and every order on my own. If I set it up correctly, the system would manage itself!

My e-commerce workflow took about a day to set up, but it was all pretty straightforward. I had to link my PayPal account to E-junkie so that I could accept payments. I ran a test purchase when everything was ready. The trial purchase went through flawlessly. Seconds later I received an email with a link to download my ebook.

It worked.

That's when I started to get nervous.

Doubt began to enter my brain, trying to stop me from moving forward like it always does right before I do something different, something that I'm uncomfortable with, something that could actually change my life or be amazing. I had the same feeling in high school when I'd stop myself from asking a girl out because she'd probably reject me.

"Why the heck am I so afraid? Why am I always stopping myself? Why am I my own worst enemy?"

I started to think about the worst things that could happen if I were to launch the ebook on my site. I immediately imagined death or lying cold and naked in a ditch somewhere, but that was stupid.

There goes my brain again.

After the anxiety subsided, I started to think reasonably about the worst thing that could happen. I surprised myself when I figured out that the worst-case scenario was not selling any books.

That was it; the worst that could happen was zero sales.

I weighed my options: Do I stick the buy now code on the website and possibly sell nothing? Or do I stop here after all that I've done and wonder what could have been?

The decision was a no-brainer. It was time to be brave and start taking a chance on myself.

IT WAS WEDNESDAY, October 1. I'd spent all night working on a sales page for my ebook. I Photoshopped a makeshift cover with the title of the book so I could include it on the page. Then I got the code from E-junkie for my ebook and pasted it on my website, causing the buy now button to appear. Finally, after hours and hours of work, everything was ready to go. I hovered my cursor over the publish button, paused, then clicked. The page refreshed, and the sales page was live.

Deep breath.

I added links to the sales page to the top and bottom of my website, then looked at the clock.

Three a.m.

I had to get up for work in a couple of hours, so I immediately shut down the computer and went to bed.

· · · · ·

FOUR HOURS LATER, I was on a train headed to work. No sales yet, but it was still early. I wasn't worried, just tired. Probably too tired to worry.

At eight a.m. I walked into the deserted office. The emptiness was sad to experience every day. So, in a way, I was thankful I only had until the end of the month before I was officially laid off and wouldn't have to come back. The temporary paycheck was the only thing keeping me there.

I sank into my chair, fired up my computer, and immediately checked to see if I had made any sales.

ZERO.

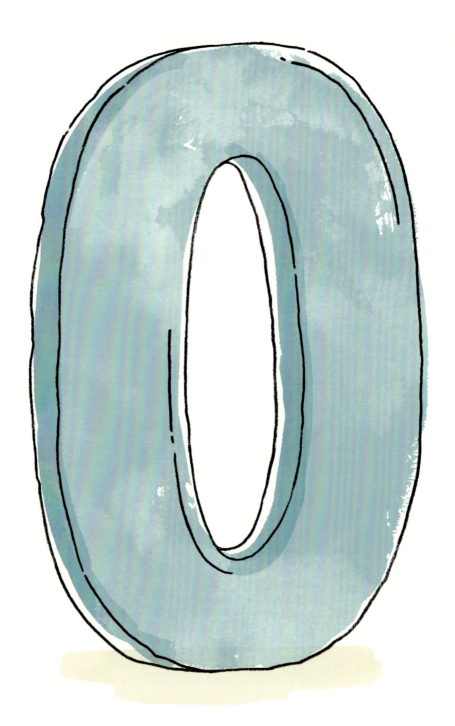

I felt a little deflated, but it was still early. I had to be realistic and give it some more time before officially flipping out.

Then, something amazing happened.

At 8:40 a.m., I received an email from PayPal with the subject line "Notification of payment received." It was for my first sale! I quickly signed into my PayPal account and there it was: a $19.99 credit from Steven for *The LEED AP Walkthrough*, by Pat Flynn.

I wanted to cry. I wanted to jump on my chair and yell. I wanted to give Steven, whoever (and wherever) he was a huge hug. I was so happy.

I had to step outside and walk around a little to fathom exactly what had just happened.

I'd actually made a sale!

I was so proud of myself, more proud than when I'd landed my job as a drafter.

One sale. That's all I really wanted: the confirmation that I could do it. And I did. I really did.

When I came back to my desk fifteen minutes later, I saw another email from PayPal.

"Notification of payment received."

I couldn't believe my eyes. Another sale! And it had happened while I was out taking a walk!

I made a total of ten sales for $199.90 that day, which was more money than I had ever earned in a single day working in an architecture firm.

It was the start of a new life.

OCT

OBER

2008

OCT

JAN

UARY

2009

JAN

"The true measure of your worth includes all the benefits others have gained from your success."

Cullen Hightower

I TOOK THE TRAIN TO WORK EACH DAY FOR MY LAST FEW WEEKS.

But while my body was headed into the office, my mind was focused on my business. Sales continued to roll in as my happiness continued to rise.

Then October 21 happened: a special day that I will never forget.

It was my last day in the office and the last time I saw my co-workers.

It was my last day riding the train, which was bittersweet because as much as I hated waking up at four thirty every morning, I actually loved the scenic commute up and down the coast.

And it was a record day of sales for my business up to that point. That day I sold twenty copies of my ebook for a total of $399.80.

Most importantly, at five p.m. that day, I officially started working for myself. There were no more regular, predictable paychecks, but at the same time there was no limit to what I could earn. No more strict work hours. No more meetings. No more stupid office drama. I was on my own, and I felt free.

I felt like an entrepreneur.

BY THE END of October I had sold over three hundred copies of my ebook, which—in addition to some advertising income—earned a total of $7,906.55. That sum was double what I had been earning as a Job Captain. And the really crazy part? The sales process was almost entirely automated. The product was being sold and delivered on its own.

The business wasn't 100 percent hands-off, however, because I still had to answer emails from customers every now and then. But the emails were few and far between. And when I stopped responding to emails, the rest of the business continued to run.

My business was working for me, not the other way around.

That's the beauty of doing business online, and the reason why I chose not to sell a physical, hardcover version of my ebook. I didn't want to go to the post office after each sale.

The freedom that this kind of digital business offered me was priceless.

During the next few months, I continued to work minimal hours as my income continued to grow. In January 2009, I added an audio guide to my product line, which was just an audio version of my ebook. In that month alone, the website and its products earned a total of $19,114.13. Except for a few shopping cart and PayPal fees, virtually all of it was profit.

I was beyond grateful for the money. That level of income was more than I could have ever hoped for. April and I were still living at our parents' homes at the time. We were never the type of people to spend money beyond what we needed to live and enjoy life. Thanks to my newfound business, we knew we were going to be okay and began planning to move into an apartment together immediately after our wedding in February.

Even more incredible than the money was the barrage of thank you emails, comments, and a few handwritten notes that I received from

NO MORE STRICT WORK HOURS. NO MORE MEETINGS. NO MORE STUPID OFFICE DRAMA. I WAS ON MY OWN, AND I FELT FREE.

customers and readers who had used my material to pass the LEED exam. My inbox received dozens of emails every single day thanking me for everything that I was doing. This was proof that I was actually helping people, people who cared enough about my help to take the time to personally thank me for it. I even received a number of emails from readers who had already passed the exam before my ebook came out but who ended up buying it anyway, just to say thanks.

That sincere gratitude meant everything to me.

Every building has an architect who designed it, but nobody ever thinks about who that person was. Most people don't even care. And

there I was, earning more money than I ever had before and getting thanked by thousands of people, by name, for sharing my knowledge and experience with a little exam that I'd taken, ironically, to advance on the corporate path.

One day I struck up a conversation with a customer after thanking him for his purchase. We started talking about my job situation and how upset I was when I was laid off. He was genuinely sorry about the news, but then he wrote me the following:

"Keep your head high, and thank your former employer for taking the chains off your potential."

That was the moment when I realized that getting laid off was actually a blessing in disguise. My job had been clouding my vision of not only what was possible in business but also what was possible for me.

From that point forward my vision was crystal clear: I wasn't on someone else's predetermined path; I was out there creating my own.

•   •   •   •   •

MOST PEOPLE WORRY when life doesn't go 100 percent according to plan. Instead, you should worry when it does. Plans are good and necessary to have, but they shouldn't be written in stone. Be open to and welcoming of unforeseen events, because those unplanned moments are often the seeds of spectacular opportunities in your life.

Imagine watching a movie where nothing challenging ever happens to any of the characters. How boring! Stories new and old teach us that the unexpected is what makes life interesting. And although you may be disappointed, disheartened, or disoriented for moments of your life, those moments happen to make you a stronger person and your life a better, more fulfilling story.

The best thing to do is just let go.

FEBRUARY 2009 TO 2013

"Family is not an important thing. It's every-thing."

Michael J. Fox

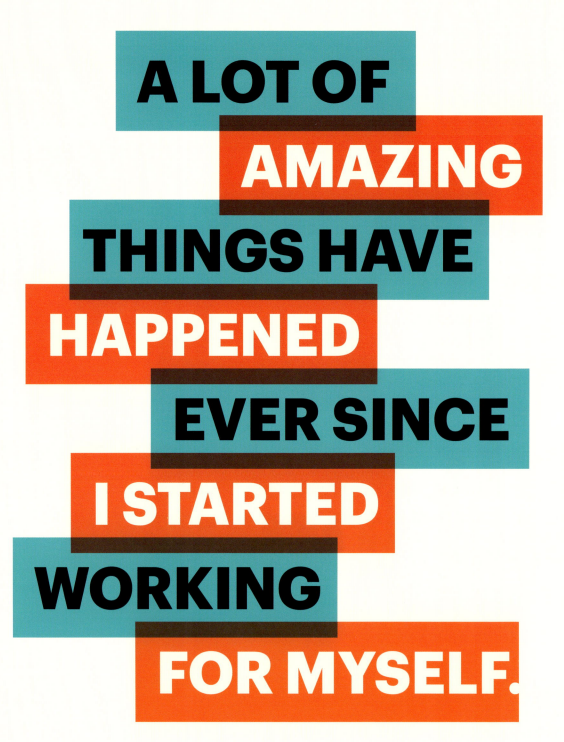

A LOT OF AMAZING THINGS HAVE HAPPENED EVER SINCE I STARTED WORKING FOR MYSELF.

MOST IMPORTANTLY, I've been able to spend most of my time with my family. April and I were married in February 2009 and she continues to be my biggest supporter. Without her encouragement and belief in me I don't even know what life would be like right now.

We had our son, Keoni, in December of the same year. Because I work from home I've witnessed all of his firsts: his first smile, his first laugh, his first steps, and his first words. Also, his first tantrum, his first bite of pizza, his first swim, his first everything! I wouldn't trade any of those memories for the world. We recently had our second child, Kailani, in September 2012. I plan to be there for all of her firsts too. Everything I do is for my children.

In May 2009, my LEED exam business surpassed $100,000 in sales. I went on to finish the year with over $203,000 in earnings and about $175,000 in total profit. In 2013 I earned between $40,000 and $50,000 per month from various online businesses I own. My dad, who wanted me to go back to school after my layoff, is now my biggest fan. He never mentioned grad school again. And he's always excited to talk about what I do online.

I also started a new blog at SmartPassiveIncome.com (SPI) with the intention of sharing everything that I learned (and continue to learn) about online business. I do this for free so that others can understand the options that are available to them without the hype or pressure to buy anything. SPI is my way of giving back for all of the amazing things that have happened to me ever since being let go. In August 2012, *Forbes* recognized me as one of the top ten transparent leaders in business.

SPI currently welcomes millions of visitors per year. I host an accompanying podcast, available on iTunes and Stitcher, that was featured in the *New York Times*, has had over 2.5 million downloads, and is consistently ranked as one of the top ten business podcasts on iTunes.

ONE LAST STORY

"Whether success or failure, I want the satisfaction of knowing my results are my own."

Pat Flynn

I have one more quick story to tell you.

In June 2009, I got an out-of-the-blue phone call from my ex-boss, the one who had told me I was going to be let go almost exactly a year before. It was really nice to hear from him; he's a good man. We exchanged some small talk at first. Then I learned that the sister office I'd left behind in Irvine had folded at the beginning of the year. I also learned that he'd started his own architecture firm in the area with a few of the others from the office who had been let go too. They were continuing to work with some of the clients that they'd been working with when the office closed.

"That's cool," I said. "I'm glad you and the others are still able to find work to do."

Then my boss cut to the chase.

"Pat, the main reason I called is because I want you to come back and work for me. I have a spot for you in the new office and you can start as soon as you can get up here. I'll start you at your Job Captain salary and even pay for your move from wherever you're located now."

It didn't take me long to reply.

"Thanks, but no thanks. I'm doing pretty well now, but thank you for your offer."

It was the most satisfying "no" I've ever said in my life.

LET-TING GO, BY, CHOICE

THE MOMENT

"I needed to let go of the way I had been doing things."

Pat Flynn

"DUDE, YOU'VE GOT TO START TREATING YOUR COMPANY LIKE YOU'RE THE CEO."

That's what Ramit Sethi said to me on a Skype call in late 2013.

You may know Ramit as the author of *I Will Teach You To Be Rich*, as well as a no-nonsense guide to entrepreneurs everywhere. The moment I heard him say those words was the moment everything changed, the moment when it clicked: I'm the CEO of my business, and I need to start acting like one.

Leading up to that conversation with Ramit, I was facing challenges in my business that I didn't know how to overcome. I needed a new paradigm, a state shift of some kind. I needed to let go of the way I had been doing things and embrace a new approach to working and growing. I just didn't know what that new approach, that new mindset, might be. Despite all my success, I was struggling mightily, unsure of what to do next.

Okay, you're probably wondering how I got here.

I'll tell you.

WHEN I STARTED out in online business in 2008, my motivation was survival. I had recently been laid off. I wanted to find something that could get me back to the point I had been financially before I lost my job. My success with GreenExamAcademy.com exceeded that benchmark, so I was very lucky to have stumbled upon that opportunity.

But I also know that I succeeded because I took action: I saw an opportunity, and acted on it. After GreenExamAcademy.com, I saw that I could do this entrepreneur thing, that this new path I was on could work. I also saw that it was something I was probably going to be doing for the rest of my life. At that point, I switched out of survival mode and into something different. I began to ask myself: How can I build this business in a way that can help me thrive? How can I take the business to a point where I no longer feel financially insecure? I wanted to get to a place where I could be confident in my skills and what I was doing, and to realize that my first experience with online business success wasn't just a flash in the pan.

A few years later, I was thriving, and setting my sights higher than ever. My email list had grown to more than fifty thousand people. I started experimenting with new business ideas, including a podcast. Smart Passive Income was turning into a huge brand and platform, and people were starting to see me as a leader who they could trust in the online entrepreneurship space. The success and visibility were pushing me onward, and I was constantly looking for ways to reach more people and have an even bigger impact.

Things were going great. Or so it seemed. The truth was that despite my success, there were many parts of the business that weren't going so well. When you start to grow your business and build fans, a lot of people want your attention and time; they want answers to their questions. As a result, my email inbox was growing out of control. At one point, I was closing in on ten thousand unread emails. I used to be able to reply to every single email, every blog comment, and every social media message—and then all of a sudden I couldn't keep up. Whenever I opened my email inbox, I'd say to myself, "This is crazy!" Every single email felt like another inevitable letdown for the person who had sent it, because I knew I wasn't going to be able to reply.

That awful feeling of not being able to respond, not serve my audience anymore, hit me in my gut every time. I knew it wasn't supposed to be this way. I knew there were people out there who were actually able to manage their email—I just didn't know where to begin to solve the problem.

I was also falling behind with my editorial calendar, thanks (or no thanks) to the recent addition of two podcasts to go along with my blog and YouTube channel. By 2011, I wasn't publishing content regularly on those two channels because I couldn't find the time. The blog content started to slow way down, and I hadn't posted a video on my YouTube channel in years. I was still going strong with the podcast, but it was taking a lot of time since I was doing so much of the editing and production work myself.

I had a great audience, but I knew I wasn't serving them in the best way possible. Many of my friends and peers were launching courses, coming out with new, cool products, holding their own events, and doing all sorts of other exciting things. Taking the leap to create things like that was simply something I couldn't imagine. I felt behind, like things were just moving too slowly, and I was starting to get buried by my business. I wondered if maybe I wasn't supposed to own a business, that I'd just gotten lucky.

As these friends and peers started surpassing me, I was proud of them, but in the back of my mind I also felt like maybe I wasn't doing what I was supposed to be doing. A good example of that was John Lee Dumas. He had created a podcast, *Entrepreneurs on Fire*, in 2012, and his income reports had started to far outshine mine. Playing the comparison game is never good, but seeing how John was running his business showed me how I could have done things differently if I had thought about my business in a smarter way.

Although I tried to avoid feeling jealous of John, watching him succeed really drove me. I didn't want to *be* him, but seeing what he was doing spurred me to think, "How can I be more strategic? How can I be more purposeful with what I do?"

But that next level seemed out of reach. I knew I wanted more, but I didn't know how to get there. I felt like an amateur, like I was creating things as I was going, but I wasn't creating the *path*—only following it. As a result of this lack of sense of control, my state of mind wasn't great. I was anxious, making decisions in a reactionary way. At the worst points, things felt like they were spinning out of control. Even though the business was growing and my income was growing, deep down I knew that something was going to break. I had to make a decision, to change my approach, but I didn't know what that might be.

· · · · ·

TYPICALLY, WHEN PEOPLE get to that point, one of three things will happen. The first is that they burn out. My good friend Chris Ducker experienced that in 2010, becoming so overworked trying to grow his business and keep a hand in every aspect of things that he ended up in the hospital. He got through it, thankfully, but I knew from seeing him suffer that I definitely didn't want that to happen to me.

My second option was to try to maintain the status quo—to settle, and find a way to make things work more or less the way they had been going. I might continue to feel overworked, but maybe, if I kept my ambitions in check, I could avoid burning out too badly. This option felt like more of a possibility than the first one did. I thought, "What if I just kind of stay where I'm at?" The business had continued to grow, I was still making money, and on the outside nothing was really broken.

I could have stayed in place, bringing in revenue and maintaining the business the way it was . . . or so I thought. Somewhere inside me, I knew that this route wouldn't work either. It would stunt my growth. I would eventually plateau—or worse, I'd start to slide toward mediocrity, and the quality and consistency of everything I did would suffer. Plus, deep down, I knew that the status quo wasn't good enough, that I already wasn't doing my best to serve my audience. The way it was all happening just didn't feel right in my gut. Keeping things as they were wasn't going to work, and I knew I had to figure some things out.

That brought me to option three: to let go of the idea that I could do everything myself and find a new way of approaching things. I knew that in order to get out of this dilemma so I could help more people and grow the business—and to be totally honest, continue to make more money—I needed to find people who knew what they were doing and who could help me understand how to do the same thing for my own business.

So I started reaching out. Thankfully, I had a great network I could turn to, and I began to share my my predicament with several of my peers and mentors. I turned to Chris Ducker, and a few other key people who had helped me along the way. I started sharing my struggles, and got a lot of good advice and feedback.

Some of that feedback opened my eyes to crucial changes I needed to make. For one, it hammered home the importance of building a team around me that could carry some of the load and free me up to work on higher-level stuff. Other advice I got, although well-meaning, was a little too tactical to get me where I needed to be. ("Put an FAQ on your site!") I was taking steps in the right direction, but there was still a bigger piece missing, something I couldn't put my finger on, that might help me shift my frame of thinking about everything.

My conversation with Ramit came toward the end of my tailspin, as my troubles seemed to be spiraling. It's a cliché to say it happened at just the right moment—I think there are plenty of potential "right moments"—but his advice definitely arrived at a time when I was ready to hear it.

Ramit is somebody who has inspired me over the years—and continues to. His blog was one of the first I ever subscribed to. He taught me the power of the small win, a concept that was huge for me when I was starting out and trying to build momentum in my young business. Although he was someone I held in high esteem and had been following for years, he also wasn't somebody I had immediate access to. He and I had met a couple of times, but we hadn't talked much on those occasions.

Thankfully, it took a simple email to set up our conversation. In late 2013, we grabbed an hour to talk over Skype. In our conversation, Ramit laid down the proverbial law and told me I needed to start thinking less like a business owner and more like a CEO. What he meant was this: I needed to get smart about where my time was going, about how money was being spent, about who I hired . . . about everything, basically. I needed to let go of not just some of the roles and responsibilities I had taken on in my business, but of the *identity* I had created for myself over the years. I needed to let go of the story I had been telling myself about who I was when it came to my business.

While others were offering well-intended and sometimes even helpful advice, it was that one line—*you need to start treating your business like you're the CEO*—that brought things into sharp clarity. That line showed me that I need to start thinking about my business not as a scrappy little thing that I'd put together, Frankenstein-like, over the years, but as a thing that needed to be treated with care and respect.

That line, and that conversation, planted the seed that would change my approach to my business. It opened me up to embrace the mindset of a CEO. It invited me to let go of some of the limiting beliefs that had been guiding my decisions for so long. It offered the shift I needed to continue to serve my audience, grow the business, and to feel like I was thriving again.

EVEN BEFORE THE crisis phase, there were other shifts that had been taking place for a while and pushing me to a point of recognizing that something big needed to change. A huge one was family, particularly the birth of my firstborn son, Keoni, at the end of 2009.

After Keoni arrived on the scene, everything in my life "leveled up" in terms of importance. I wanted to support my family and be a good father and husband, and there was obviously the added financial constraint of having a child. I started to think more about my future, and the future I was creating for my son. Everything started to feel a little more urgent.

As a result, I knew I had to be even more serious about what I was doing with my business. So I became super efficient. I knew that every second I wasted—whether down a YouTube rabbit hole or on social media—was time taken away from my son and my wife. I was motivated to get things done efficiently, and I looked more closely at how I was spending my time. I became laser-focused on efficiency and productivity: getting more of the important things done, faster. I was constantly aware of how I chose to spend my time, and what it was actually doing for me.

Then in 2012, my second child, Kailani, was born. Her arrival was yet another reminder of the stakes. At that point, Keoni was two years old and starting to become a little more self-sufficient—but all of a sudden, here was another new person in the mix, and it was back to square one with the time and care required. Out of the frying pan and into the fire, as they say.

In 2011 I started speaking at conferences, and by 2012 I was spending a lot of time traveling to those events. As a result, I was far from home for long periods. I struggled with finding a balance between the time I spent running my business and being a father and husband. In September 2012, I was scheduled to speak at FinCon, a huge annual financial content exposition, but Kailani ended up being born on the same day, a whole month before her due date. Missing Kailani's birth would have been much worse than missing the exposition. At that point I started to realize even more clearly how important my time was, and where I needed to spend it.

After Kailani was born, although the speaking opportunities kept coming in, I began saying no to way more opportunities than I said yes to. More than ever, I wanted to be home with my family. As the family continued to grow and my business got busier, the unexpected timing of Kai's birth was a reminder of the things that were the most important to me. It was a reminder of how precious our time really is. Kai may have been born a month early, but I think she came at the perfect time.

Finding a way to balance the challenges of running a business and raising a new baby was one thing. But another element that was a little tougher for me was taking care of my health. Basically, I had been prioritizing my business and my family over my own well-being. With the demands of a new baby, health and fitness took a backseat and by 2009, not long after Keoni was born, I had let myself go. I got to the point where I'd look at pictures of myself and be disappointed with what I saw. Plus, I was tired all the time. I remember going up the stairs one day holding Keoni. He only weighed about ten pounds, and it was only one set of stairs, but the effort tired me out. I said to myself, "This can't happen."

So I started to focus more on my workout training. I picked up P90X. I started to feel better, look better, and feel more confident, which was great. But then in 2012, it was like déjà vu all over again. After Kailani was born, the same thing happened: I began to let my health get away from me. That's when I started to dive into nutrition. I had determined by that point that what I was putting in my body, more than what I was doing in terms of physical fitness, was having the biggest effect on my overall health.

Dialing in my fitness regimen, and then my nutrition, helped get me back to where I had been health- and energy-wise before each of the kids was born. I'm thankful that I was able to learn from those experiences. I'm also thankful that through all the stress of building and running a business and supporting my family, I've never had a real health scare. Along the way, I've had to make changes and find new tools, better ways to balance work life and family life. The worst things I've encountered health-wise have been frustrating reminders of the importance of being healthy—things like huffing and puffing while I haul a toddler up the stairs. I've seen others, like my good friend Chris Ducker, push themselves into a full-on health crisis by working too hard. Thankfully, I've stayed away from that scary edge, but I still know that no matter how exciting my ambitions might be, my health is more important. Without it, I'm not much use to anyone.

· · · · ·

THE PAST FEW years have given me a great opportunity to understand what motivates me—and what doesn't. One thing I've learned along the way is that material things don't motivate me very much, and to be honest, they never really have. Even though I could afford fancy, expensive things if I wanted them, I've realized that they don't matter that much in the grand scheme.

That said, I think it's okay to reward yourself from time to time, as long as it's something you'll truly appreciate. I bought myself a Tesla Model X last year, as a reward for a successful year. Every time I drive it, I'm reminded of how far I've come, and of the work that I've put in. This reward helps keep me grounded and makes sure that I stay true to myself, because the work I've done, and the path I've taken, has brought me to where I am today.

What's more important to me than material rewards is keeping my family safe, and providing them with amazing experiences and memories. It's also being a guide for others who might want to follow a similar path to mine. I've always been motivated to be a leader, but I also know what kind of leader I don't want to be. I've never wanted to be a guru. I've never wanted to be the guy on the top of the mountain who thinks he knows everything and is simply yelling it down at everyone else. I would rather lead by example. That's why I try to be honest about my failures and share them openly with my audience. I want my personal lessons to be lessons for everybody, and I think that's a big reason I've been able to grow trust with such a large audience.

It's just a part of who I am: somebody who wants to lead and serve people, but who doesn't want to be above everyone else. I sometimes think of myself as the guy in the forest who's holding the machete, who can clear the path for others. I might be the one who is in the most danger—maybe I'll come across a jaguar along the way—but at least I can protect people up front using the weapons that I have.

I've also never wanted to be a leader who just talks the talk. I want to be somebody who can back up my claims and make decisions that let me sleep at night. With growth and exposure comes a lot of opportunities that can be very attractive when it comes to commission and fame. I get dozens of emails every week from people who want the opportunity to get in front of my audience, and who offer me incredible rewards for that opportunity. But I know that if I were to go down that route, I would begin to lose my audience's trust, and it wouldn't be worth it.

There's a line I think about a lot, especially when I'm faced with business decisions that might involve a moral cost: "With great audiences comes great responsibility." My audience keeps me grounded so that I can make the right call in these kinds of situations. My family, and especially my kids, are a big influence for me too, in terms of how I lead by example. With two young kids in the house now, I think a lot about the legacy I'm creating for them, about the impression they'll have of me, and the choices I make in my life and business.

When you're thinking about embarking down a new path, let the people you serve and the legacy you want to create be your guiding light for the decisions you make. Don't favor short-term gains at the expense of the long term. Be sure that whatever you're building is something you will be proud of twenty, thirty, forty years from now—and something your audience, your family, and anyone else who matters to you, will be proud of you for creating, too.

THE MINDSET

> **Despite all of my success, I was doing things in an amateur way.**
>
> Pat Flynn

HAVING RAMIT TELL ME I NEEDED TO ACT MORE LIKE A CEO WAS THE CATALYST I NEEDED TO MAKE SOME BIG CHANGES.

But after I hung up with him that day in 2013, I immediately thought, "I don't know anything about being a CEO." I was having a hard time wrapping my head around the idea." CEO. Okay. Does that mean I have to dress up in a suit and go into an office every day?"

I knew that because of how I had been running the business to that point, it wasn't growing as fast as I wanted it to and I was letting people down. Despite all of my success, I was doing things in an amateur way. On the plus side, there was no doubt the conversation with Ramit had inspired me. It had given me hope that there was a path through this dilemma. But I was still harboring some big doubts, including one that seemed even more depressing: Does being CEO mean I can't be connected to my audience anymore?

Before that conversation, to me a CEO was somebody who sat at the top of the business, someone who was too important to talk to *The*

People. I did know that, no matter what, I always wanted to be serving my audience. I didn't want to mold myself into the CEO of IBM, someone far removed from the people my company serves. Not that there's anything wrong with being the CEO of IBM, of course—but Smart Passive Income is not IBM. Despite my worries, I knew that whatever I did as a next step couldn't involve abandoning my audience.

I didn't want to be that kind of CEO—but over time I came to see that I didn't have to be. One of the biggest things I've realized is that even though I've had to let go of a lot of things as CEO, there are things I haven't had to let go of, and my audience is the biggest one.

Once Ramit had introduced me to the idea of becoming a CEO, I didn't turn into one overnight. I started by determining exactly where my time was being spent, trying to better understand all the operations of my business, and building a team that could help me achieve my goals. Then, I began to deconstruct the CEO idea a little bit, and to shape it into something that would work for me and my business.

It's taken time and a lot of growth and trial and error to get to that place, but through this sometimes arduous process, I've pieced together my own version of the CEO role, one that's meaningful for me and my business. Instead of just "playing CEO," I've become a CEO in a way that makes sense for me.

It's taken time and experience to cultivate a CEO mindset and put it into action—and in a big way, that's what this book is about. The following chapters go over some of the trials and challenges that forged me in the fire, so to speak, as well as the methods and mechanics involved in building a business around a CEO mindset. This process has definitely involved, if not a new wardrobe, some restructuring of my priorities. To set the stage, I wanted to share the four elements that have emerged out of that process—the aspects I've come to embrace that I feel best capture the CEO mindset.

So, what does a CEO do?

1. A CEO looks into the numbers.

Numbers don't lie, and CEOs know this. From traffic to income and even time, tracking is a method by which a CEO can better understand how to adjust and decide on which actions to take. As I mentioned in the previous chapter, I've been keeping track of my income each month in my income reports, which date all the way back to October 2008. Doing this has kept me motivated and always helps me understand growth (or decline) in various elements of my business.

Unless you keep track, there's no way to know what's working and what's not. In the early days of SPI, the only numbers I looked at were traffic and income. I did a pretty good job focusing on these items, but there was one more important item related to numbers that took me a while to learn how to track: *time*. Time, even more than traffic and money, is the most important metric to monitor. Traffic numbers will go up and down, and you can always lose money and make more money. But once time is gone, it's gone.

I only wish I'd realized this much sooner. It wasn't until December 2009, when Keoni was born, that my drive to become more efficient and keep track of my time kicked in. As I talked about in *The Motivation*, the baby effect was very real for me. Our firstborn truly made me want to spend less time working and more time with him. But, because I still wanted to grow and expand my business, it was all about time and where I put my effort, as well as how well I performed.

One of my favorite exercises is to ask myself a simple question at the end of each month based on the Pareto Principle—the 80/20 rule: What was the smallest thing I did last month that gave me the biggest results? In other words, what are the 20 percent of things that I did to earn 80 percent of my results? For me, this often changes every month, and when I think of this in relation to all three of the previously mentioned factors—traffic, income, and time—it becomes very clear how

I should continue to move forward. It also helps me think about the things that didn't produce results that I should no longer do, or try to do in a different way.

A CEO learns to let go of stories that might not be true and focus on the data.

2. A CEO focuses on the future.

Not all CEOs may be as in love with the movie *Back to the Future* as I am, but if you're going to grow your company, you HAVE to think about the future—and not just what you're doing tomorrow or next week, but at least twelve months ahead of time, and hopefully more. In my early days as "boss," because I was involved in every aspect of the company, all of that work kept me so busy that it narrowed my vision to what I was doing in the short term only, and because of this I plateaued often—both in terms of the growth of my businesses and in my energy levels. I found myself, even as boss, working for my own business, instead of having the business work for me.

After expanding my team (more about that in "The Machine"), I got some great help from several people with big-picture planning; zooming out from that weekly calendar and looking three months ahead, six months ahead, and even a year ahead of schedule. Thanks to inspiration from people like Amy Porterfield, I picked up my first twelve-month wall calendar and started to color in when certain events were happening, everything from launches to speaking engagements, and even vacations with the family. This way, in one snapshot of the year, I could see exactly how things were spaced out, if events were too close together, and most importantly, if there was time for me to get out of the house with the family for a few hours or days.

Focusing on the big picture also helped me focus on upcoming day-to-day tasks, including what content I was going publish, who I was going to interview, and other things of this nature. Because I knew what was coming up, I could plan ahead and get moving on marketing and promotional efforts leading up to those events. It seriously put the entire business on a treadmill. Since using my bigger-picture, twelve-month calendar, as well as hiring my amazing editorial director, Janna, SPI has been a machine that continues to pump out quality content throughout the year regardless of what's going on in my personal life or in other facets of my business. A CEO focuses on the future, and in order to grow and keep your well-oiled machine running, and running well, you have to know what's coming so you'll know what to do next.

A CEO learns to let go of what's just ahead—or in the rearview mirror—and focus on what's coming way down the road.

3. A CEO does not do all of the work.

This one seems obvious, but it took me a while to fully appreciate and get past it. You can be your own boss but get stuck doing all of the work, and when you do all of the work, you drastically limit your ability to take the bolder actions required of a CEO to grow the company.

In the beginning, doing all of the work is typically your only option, and that's okay. When I started building my online business in 2008, I did all of the work myself. This was both for GreenExamAcademy.com, which included creating the website, publishing my first ebook study guide, and learning how to manage business finances, as well as all the work involved with the beginning of SmartPassiveIncome.com, which started later in the same year.

And you know what? I was glad to do all of that work! Actually, I couldn't have imagined it any other way. My business was my baby, and I wasn't going to let anyone else touch it. However, I waited until 2014 to focus on building my team and finding the right people to perform specific tasks for me—and that was a huge mistake. I couldn't trust others to do the work, and there was a certain amount of pride involved in doing it myself in my own special way, so I continued to edit my own podcasts, do all of the graphic design work, and even manage my own website and servers.

So what prompted my decision to finally start reaching out for help? It was a couple of things. First, when Chris Ducker is your best friend and he happens to own an outsourcing company and one of the top virtual staff providers in the world (Virtual Staff Finder), he hounds you time and time again when you're doing everything yourself. I kept saying, "I know, I know," but I never took any action. And yet it was always something that was in the back of my mind—I was just waiting for the "right time."

One thing I've learned as an entrepreneur, though, is that there is never a "right time." Typically, when you're waiting for the right time, that time has usually passed. All you can do is GO. What brought me over the edge was when I wanted to expand my business and create a new podcast called *AskPat*. After realizing what it would take to get it done, there was no way it was going to happen unless I had help from the outside. It was either that or two other options: don't do the show at all, or tap into the time I had reserved for the family.

Since family is a top priority of mine, option two was out of the question, so in order to see this project through, I'd have to get some help. The tricky thing with *AskPat* is that I was planning on it being a five-day-per-week show that would answer a voicemail question from the SPI audience, and to manage all of that by myself on top of everything else was going to be impossible. It was clear that I had to get outside help. So I did that, and in February 2014, *AskPat* launched. Since then, it's gained over six million downloads and earned over six figures in advertising revenue.

After hiring help for *AskPat*, I became addicted to finding out what else in my business could be shared with others, and a lot of amazing

things happened as a result. I found great people who could not only do a lot of the work I was doing but also do it a lot better and faster than I could. It opened up several hours a week that I could use on higher-level work and planning for the business. Even though I spent money to hire help, the return on investment made it absolutely worth it. I also don't miss the work as much as I thought I would.

I'll talk a lot more about how I set up my team in "The Machine." But one big thing I've learned, and that you can hopefully take advantage of too, is that you can start small. You don't have to go all-in at first, but you'll see that once you learn to allow others to help, whether that means outsourcing one-off projects to people overseas, or building a more permanent team for longer-term positions, it'll open up a whole new world for you, and your business will have a lot more room to grow and flourish like it should.

A CEO learns to let go of the work he or she may *want* to do but doesn't need to do.

4. A CEO understands, embraces, and overcomes the fear of missing out (FOMO).

Another big lesson learned as I grew into a CEO mindset was learning how to say no. Saying no is one of the hardest things to do, especially when you're at the beginning stages of entrepreneurship, and especially if you happen to be a people pleaser like I am. I want everyone to be happy, and for the first four years after starting my own entrepreneurial journey, I said yes to almost every opportunity that came my way.

Why do we do this? We say yes for a couple of reasons. First, we just don't want to let people down, but the bigger reason is because we don't want to miss out. FOMO is real! And it controls our decisions more than we might think. We hate to say no when an opportunity is presented because we don't think that opportunity will come our way ever again, or because we think someone else will take it before us.

It took me a while, but I finally learned what real CEOs do, and that's learn how to say no. A better way to put it is this: I learned when to say yes. Every time an opportunity comes my way, I give myself time to think about it. I weigh the pros and cons and first understand if I were to say yes, what I would actually be saying no to. The way I like to think about decisions is similar to the law of conservation of energy. This law states that energy can neither be created nor destroyed; rather, it can only be transformed from one form into another. My energy, my time, and my focus can neither be created nor destroyed. They just shift from one form to another, and so if I say yes to one opportunity, it means I'm also saying no to something else.

Eliminating the FOMO is the hardest part, but trusting yourself to make the right decisions for the company and for your own life will help guide you through those decisions. In many cases, thinking about what I would be saying no to, especially if it relates to something like my family, makes the decisions so much easier, and FOMO much less of an issue.

A CEO learns to let go of opportunities that aren't the best fit for the business.

. . . . .

TALKING TO RAMIT planted the seed that would shift my mindset. Up until that point, I knew that I wanted and needed to do things differently—I just couldn't frame or define what needed to change. I didn't have any specific examples or inspiration to draw on, and I just couldn't wrap my head around the idea.

After that conversation, I had a starting point, but I also saw that I still had a lot to learn. I had been set on a new learning journey, and as part of that journey, I started to see the CEO mindset in more places, especially among my peers who had been growing their businesses for longer than I had. It was almost like a veil had been pulled back and I could see what was making these people and their businesses tick.

A lot of those leaders were people I admired greatly, and one of them was Michael Hyatt. In 2013, I was invited to speak at Michael's very first Platform Conference. The conference was a great experience in all respects. But there was one aspect of the conference that tripped me out. During one of the speaking events, I saw Michael sitting in the audience, listening to the speakers who were up on stage. Throughout the conference, he would go up on the stage and speak every once in a while, but most of the time he was simply sitting in the audience and learning.

I had never seen that at any of the other conferences I'd been to previously. The person whose name was on the billboard was just sitting in the audience like a regular, paying attendee? At his own event? It blew my mind a little bit. So *who*, I wondered, *is* running the show? I was scratching my head, trying to figure out who was keeping things running smoothly behind the scenes, since it wasn't Michael. But *somebody* was, and there sat Michael, taking full advantage of some set of efficiencies I couldn't yet imagine.

I approached Michael after one of the sessions and asked him, "Hey, how are you able to do this? Wouldn't you normally be behind the scenes and freaking out, or getting things together with the program?" What he said shocked me. "No, my team's handling all that."

Michael had set up his team and the entire event so he didn't have to run around the whole time like a chicken with his head cut off. On the contrary, he could free himself up to be learning and taking in all of the awesome knowledge being shared. It inspired me to consider how I would build my own team, and more than that, how I could empower them to run things so I could focus on the bigger picture—and maybe even sit back and learn a few things while I was at it.

Michael's example showed me how important it was to build a team. In fact, Michael's Platform Conference team was probably the most amazing team I've ever seen in action. It was obvious he had put the right people in place to help him run his event—and his business—smoothly.

What that experience showed me is that being CEO is about more than building a team; it's more than creating a system in which the CEO doesn't have to have his or her hands in every part of the process. It's about creating a system in which the CEO *can't and shouldn't* be involved in everything. That separation is by design. And it's how the magic can happen.

· · · · ·

I'VE HAD—AND CONTINUE to have—many great mentors, people who've helped me see how I could do things bigger, better, and faster, and help even more people. These mentors have taught me how to be smarter about where my time is spent, as well as how to build a team, plan for the future, and understand what's actually moving the needle.

Speaking of mentors, there's another thing I learned from Ramit after our conversation in 2013, and it's something that's stuck with me: "What got you here, won't get you there." In "The Moment," I talked about the hazard of settling. Because what might seem like settling is actually moving backward. Complacency can be dangerous.

If you were to distill the four parts of being a CEO—looking at the numbers, not doing all the work, overcoming FOMO, and looking toward the future—I think you'd come up with the idea that being a CEO is about *running toward change and embracing it.* As CEO, I'm always evolving, always changing, always trying new things. You have to keep pushing forward, and questioning what you're doing even if it seems like it's working for you. And if you're not happy with where you're at right now, and things aren't working, you *definitely* can't continue to do the same things.

You know what they say about the definition of *insanity: It's doing the same thing over and over, expecting different results.*

THE MADNESS

"Slowly and surely, my fear and anxiety turned to relief and gratitude."

Pat Flynn

SINCE LEAP-
ING INTO A
WHOLE NEW
LIFE AFTER
MY LAYOFF
IN 2009,

the madness has come in many forms. What is **the madness?** It's the churn, the drama, the chaos, that's often unexpected and that forces you to react, evaluate, make decisions, make changes—and yes, let go—in ways that you might not expect, and at times when you might not want to deal with it.

I could fill a book with examples of the madness, but I chose a few to illustrate how these episodes of unanticipated trouble have led me to important realizations about the importance of embracing a CEO mindset.

The first episode came shortly after I was let go from my architecture job. In May 2009, my GreenExamAcademy.com business started accelerating, and things were going well. But it all came to a screeching halt when I received a cease-and-desist letter in the mail from the United States Green Building Council (USGBC), the organization that develops and administers the LEED exam.

I took one glance at the letter and threw my hands up: "I'm not cut out for this, I thought. Let me go find another architecture job."

After hyperventilating for a bit, I found a random attorney on Google and called him. He went over the details of the letter with me and explained that the USGBC was only asking me to stop using "LEED"—their trademark—in the domain name of my site. You see, before it was GreenExamAcademy.com, the site was called InTheLEED.com—catchy, right? But the USGBC wasn't too happy about me making money on a site that used their trademark, and they wanted me to change the name within seven days.

My lawyer called the USGBC's attorney and was able to get us a few extra days to change the domain name. But I was out of my depth in terms of how to make that happen. I found a web developer who helped me set up a new domain name and do what's called a 301 permanent redirect, which routed the old domain name to the new one. The redirect made sure we wouldn't lose our search ranking in Google.

This was the first real scare of my new business life. The whole situation had felt like a huge downward spiral from the start. Even after I'd found an attorney and started to address the problem, I struggled to maintain my composure. But slowly and surely, my fear and anxiety turned to relief and gratitude once I realized I wasn't going to lose my site and my business over this.

Then, a week later, I got another letter from the USGBC. This one basically said, "Sorry! You can't do a 301 redirect because you're still using the old domain name." I thought, "Come on, Universe! Are you out to get me right now?" I didn't understand why the USGBC would still be on my case when I was arguably helping them by encouraging people to pay hundreds of dollars to take their exam. What I later found out though, was that a number of other sites with "LEED" in their domain names had been popping up that were helping people study for the LEED exam. They were all infringing on the trademark—and most of them weren't very good—so the USGBC was cracking down on all of them, my site included.

This struggle was my first big madness moment—and a real eye-opener. My first reaction when confronted with the problem was to retreat, because I'd never had to deal with anything like this before. I grew a lot stronger out of that first big challenge, even though I wanted to give up at first. The situation showed me that I don't know everything, and that I have to surround myself with people with skills and knowledge I don't have, so they can help me when I'm out of my depth. I've been working with the same attorney now for the last eight years, and I've built a team of other excellent people who fill in the gaps that I can't fill myself (more about that in "The Machine"). I'm a lot more conscious now about when I need to call in the "SWAT team."

. . . . .

WHEN THE DOMAIN name episode happened, I explored a kind of letting go that would have been inadvisable for someone in my position—and by that, I mean the "jumping off a cliff" kind of letting go. But I've realized since then that I don't know everything, and I also don't *need* to know everything. Through experience, and building a team that can take some of the load, I haven't once thought about giving up and quitting my entrepreneurial path entirely since that episode.

Later that year, though, the madness returned: the Green Building Council came for me again. Well, not really—but it sure felt that way at first. For context, for a long time the USGBC didn't provide their own study guides for the LEED exam. Then all of a sudden in 2009, they decided to create their own guides. When I found out, I was terrified. I thought my business would have to shut down. Why would people buy a guide from me when they could buy one from the very same people who wrote the exam questions?

I thought I was done for.

But instead, something interesting happened, and the madness shifted to something pleasantly surprising. Shortly after the USGBC released their study guides, I had a record sales month. I didn't understand what was going on. Why would my sales be increasing now that there's *more* competition for my product?

I couldn't figure it out, so I decided to survey my audience to see if I could learn more. I started asking new study guide customers why they had purchased my guide. The responses were eye-opening. Most of them mentioned the USGBC guide, but all of them said that they'd bought from me anyway because they felt like they knew me. They could relate to me as somebody who had taken the exam not too long ago, as somebody who was just a few steps ahead of them. One of the cool things I noticed about their responses was that they all said, "Hey Pat," or, "Thanks, Pat." It wasn't, "Hey, GreenExamAcademy.com," or, "Thanks, GreenExamAcademy.com." It was Pat. They were able to feel a personal connection with me.

These responses helped me understand my unique selling proposition—what attracted those people to buy from me instead of someone else. I went from being scared of the competition and feeling like the USGBC was offering something more valuable than what I could provide, to seeing things in a totally different light.

After that record sales month, I decided to invest some of the money into new business ideas. I came up with a list of ten ideas and showed them to my mentor, Jeremy, from *Internet Business Mastery*, to get his reactions.

After looking at all of them, he said to me, "Pat, these businesses are pretty cool. They're really good ideas, but there's one thing missing from all of them."

"What's that?" I asked him. "What's the one thing?"

"You. Your personality's not in here. You have this incredible ability to connect with people online and to build their trust. If you don't bake that into your ideas, it's going to be harder to succeed, because you won't be utilizing your superpower."

With GreenExamAcademy.com, I shared how I struggled on the exam and didn't get a perfect score. Because of that, people trusted me and knew that my experience was real, which led them to purchase from me and not the other guys. Meanwhile, although Smart Passive Income had been up and running and doing well at that point, I had been reluctant to share as much of myself on that site.

Despite the feedback I got from my study guide customers, I hadn't quite internalized the lesson. But with Jeremy's input, I knew how powerful it could be to inject myself even more into the SPI brand. So I started being open about the fact that we were having kids. I hired a voiceover guy to share a random fun fact about me at the beginning of every episode of my podcast. Now, every time I go to a conference and meet someone new, the two of us can immediately have a conversation like longtime friends, before I even know their name. All because they already know these things about me.

Whatever I do now, I always try to capitalize on the unique angle that differentiates me from others, so that once the competition arrives, I know that I'm still going to be okay—and maybe even do better—because I know my unique selling point: Pat.

•   •   •   •   •

EARLY 2013: I was in San Francisco with my videographer, Caleb Wojcik, to shoot on-location interviews and stories that were going to be used in the first edition of *Let Go*. (You can check them out at patflynn.com/letgo-videos/). During a break in shooting, I took a few minutes to visit my website to read the comments on a blog post I had just written.

Instead, I found a server error.

No big deal, I thought. I'd had server errors before, and things were typically back up and running in fifteen minutes to an hour. I left a message on social media letting people know the site was temporarily down, and Caleb and I went about our day like normal. Two or three hours later, it was still down. I was getting a little concerned at this point, so I started a web chat with my server hosting company. They told me that the site was under a denial of service (DOS) attack. And it wasn't just SmartPassiveIncome.com that had been targeted; five or six other websites of mine that were hosted on the same server were also completely down.

The hosting company said they would look into it and resolve the problem. I thanked them and closed the chat, but my concern lingered. I was supposed to be on point, shooting videos, but all I could think about was the website. A couple hours later, I checked again. It was still down, so I followed up with the hosting company again. No luck yet. It was nighttime by that point, so I was hoping that by the morning it would all be resolved. I sent another update on social media, and an email out to my list, thanking them for their patience. By then, I was also receiving hundreds of emails from people saying, "Hey, your site's down."

(Yeah, I know.)

I woke up the next day, and the site was still down. This attack had been a fierce one. Someone had clearly targeted me and my sites. It felt kind of incredible to me that I was somebody worth targeting. I didn't understand why someone would choose to do something like that, but it also made me think, "Well, I guess I'm big-time now if people are doing this."

At the same time, the hosting company didn't seem to be putting a lot of effort into fixing the problem, and I was getting frustrated. After several more days of anxiety, web chats, and phone calls, they were able to get the sites back up. After all was said and done, the whole thing took a week to resolve.

The attack made me realize that my website was vulnerable. Immediately after my site was back up, I switched hosting companies and hired someone to help me with site security to make sure it wouldn't happen again. I also ended up losing about $15,000 to $20,000 in affiliate commissions from the downtime. I was able to recoup a few thousand dollars from an insurance policy, but I still lost a lot of time on the phone, signing papers and delivering evidence to the insurance company. It was a huge hassle, and almost not worth it.

I was thankful I'd had insurance, but I also realized that the bigger insurance in this fiasco was my audience—and specifically, my email list. I was able to, through that whole week, update and communicate with people. And worst case, even if my site had never come back, I could have "set up shop" again somewhere else and things would have been fine, because I'd have had access to my audience. On the other hand, if I hadn't had my email list, I'd have been completely lost. I would have been done.

·   ·   ·   ·   ·

SOMETHING THAT'S inevitable as you start to succeed and gain visibility is that you're going to be targeted. The USGBC had targeted me, although thankfully they had no ill intentions. The SmartPassive Income.com hackers had targeted me, and they *did* have ill intentions. But you could argue that they weren't out to get *me*, Pat Flynn.

Now, I'm a people-first person. I want to help as many others as I possibly can. And I have always welcomed feedback from people who want to offer respectful, constructive criticism. That's an important thing any business owner should welcome, because it's a piece of the voice of your audience, one that helps you grow and improve. But as I started to grow and gain more exposure, I also started to attract a number of people who were blatantly targeting me or people in my community in a disrespectful manner—haters, trolls, and bullies.

In 2010 and 2011, the haters and trolls began to arrive, especially as SmartPassiveIncome.com became more popular. One day I did a web search for my name and came across a note in a forum where someone referred to me as "pond scum." This person argued that I was "fake" and my income numbers weren't real.

Like the USGBC letter, it stopped me in my tracks. I quit working for about a week, and experienced a lot of anxiety and pain. I didn't know who this person was, and I knew I wasn't pond scum, but I was starting to believe it a little bit. Why? Because someone was willing to say it, and not just to me, but in an open forum where others could see it, too.

After a week of fretting, I decided to do something. I would respond, and I was going to take the high road. As I was formulating my response strategy, I took some inspiration from Gary Vaynerchuk. After his book *Crush It* came out, Gary reached out to the people who had written one- and two-star reviews of the book, asking if he could have a conversation with them to understand why they felt that way about it.

Now, most of the people I was talking to about this issue were telling me, "Hey, just ignore it. Don't feed the trolls." And the majority of the time, I think this is good advice. (I'll get to that strategy in a minute.) But in this particular case, I knew that a simple misunderstanding was to blame, and I thought Gary's approach would be perfect for my situation. So I decided to deal with it head-on.

First, I became a member of the forum, and wrote a long post about who I was and what I was doing. Then I sent a note to the forum member who had called me "pond scum," offering to get on a Skype call to hash things out. In my note, I tried my best not to be confrontational: "Hey," I said. "There must be some misunderstanding here. I'd love to get on a chat with you and figure it out." Thankfully, the person agreed, and we found a time to chat.

In my conversation with her, I did my best not to come across as upset or angry, only inquisitive and honest. I even shared screenshots of some of my accounts to show her that I was telling the truth in my income reports. The strategy worked. A few days later, she came back and apologized on the forum. She retracted her previous statement about me, and told everyone that I was actually a caring person who was telling the truth about my business results.

I understood why she had said what she did—she saw a situation where someone (i.e., me) could potentially take advantage of others, and she wanted to protect them. I was glad she and I were ultimately able to understand each other and resolve the issue. But that wasn't the end of my hater dilemmas. In fact, they were only about to get worse.

In 2011, someone else left a lengthy comment on one of my blog posts. In the comment, which must have been almost a thousand words long, he called me all sorts of names: unqualified, a liar, a con artist, and many other hateful things. I decided at first to just ignore it. But then he started leaving the same comment on dozens of other websites. Soon, friends and colleagues were emailing me, asking what was going on.

I went back to the original comment he'd left on my website and said, "Why did you do this? I don't understand why you posted it on everybody else's site as well. Can we talk on Skype? I'd love to answer exactly where you're coming from. Maybe there's something I can do to help you." I tried to take the high road again. But I got no reply.

I was frazzled. I couldn't understand why this person was doing what he was doing. It was pure bullying, and it hurt me deeply. I started to find more and more instances of his comments, and even forums where groups of people were discussing the situation. I didn't have any energy to work. It was all I could think about. I constantly felt like throwing up.

After four or five miserable weeks, I finally tracked down the troll and reached out to him over email. Although he never agreed to talk to me, he did finally respond to my email telling me why he'd done what he did. Basically, he knew I was very popular online, and by making a big stir he thought he could drum up more traffic for his own website.

That was all it was: a traffic-generating tactic.

I was so upset. I couldn't believe someone would stoop to that level to get website visits. It also fired me up. I felt even more inspired to show people that there were legitimate ways to make money that involved being authentic and not hurting other people. And to see that this guy was taking the complete opposite approach just made me feel sorry for him.

In the wake of this episode, I had a conversation with my buddy Derek Halpern, who told me, "Every second you waste spending time thinking about a hater is a second you're taking away from those who actually care about you and need you." I had spent a month thinking nonstop about someone who had taken advantage of me—four weeks that had pulled me away from my mission of serving my audience. That realization put things into sharp perspective.

So, what should you do when you're confronted with the inevitable trolls and haters out there? How you respond depends on who you are, but in most cases, I would recommend not engaging at all. This sort of thing is never fun to deal with, but just remember that people who act this way typically represent a very, very small percentage of your audience. So don't be frazzled by it, because it's rarely a reflection on you. It never feels great, but at the same time, it's kind of cool knowing that you're worth the attention—that you're making an impact, and people are taking the time to think of you. Of course, they're not thinking about you in a positive way, but they're thinking about you nonetheless, which means you must be doing something right.

And just remember that simply by putting yourself out there, you're making yourself vulnerable. In fact, I would be a little worried if you didn't eventually have some haters, because if you're pleasing every-body, you're probably not thinking big enough. Every celebrity, every star, everyone who's done anything meaningful has had people who didn't like them. Albert Einstein had haters. Benjamin Franklin had people who disliked him. Elon Musk has people who don't like him. This stuff happens, and it's actually a good sign: *Hey, you're big enough to have haters now. That's awesome.*

· · · · ·

THE MADNESS ISN'T always a big, dramatic thing that affects your life for weeks on end. Sometimes it's more mundane, like saying yes to a podcast interview and completely missing the date. Yes, I did that once. I thought I'd put it on my calendar, but maybe I had the wrong date. Or maybe it was on the calendar, and I just missed it. Or maybe I was just too burnt out to even put it on the calendar at all. The details escape me now—but the point is, I missed it. It was one little appointment, but it was a big deal to me. Thankfully, the host was understanding, we rescheduled the interview, and everything was fine. But I didn't feel good about it. It made me realize I was having trouble being *me*. I was almost becoming a slave to my business, and I needed to start becom-ing a little smarter about what I was saying yes to.

At other times, the madness is the kind of chaos that ultimately makes you smile, that throws your priorities in sharp relief, and reminds you that your life doesn't occur in neat little boxes. We moved into a new house in 2014. At that point, both the kids were a little bit older and starting to become more independent. Working out of my home, there were often moments when I'd be recording podcasts or videos and one of the kids would come bursting into the office. This happened often enough that I would roll with it and let them be a part of it.

BUSINESS IS BUSINESS, BUT YOU HAVE TO BE WILLING TO **LET A LITTLE KID STEAL THE SHOW** FROM TIME TO TIME.

One time, Keoni came in while I was recording a podcast. He crept into my office slowly, but I saw him coming in and motioned with my hands for him to sit down near me. He sat quietly and watched me do the podcast for a good twenty minutes, until I was done recording.

Afterward he said, "Daddy, what were you doing?"

"I was recording a podcast."

"What's a podcast?"

"Oh, well, I'm talking to somebody on the other side of the world, and then we're going to share that with even more people around the world."

"Cool. Can I record a podcast?"

I got really excited about that idea, so I recorded a video interview with him. (You can find it at smartpassiveincome.com/letgo-keoni.)

There was also the time my videographer, Caleb Wojcik, came over to film for a course for my YouTube channel, SPI TV. Caleb had brought over all sorts of equipment: lights, cameras, tripods, microphones. We had just finished setting them all down in our library, when Keoni came in. He started pointing to each of them, asking, "Uncle Caleb, what's this?" Uncle Caleb would tell him, then, "Oh, cool. Uncle Caleb, what's this? Uncle Caleb, what's that?"

It was interrupting our work, but it was cute, and I liked that he was curious about it, so we went with it. It turned into a half-hour of explaining what every piece of equipment was. At the same time I realized, "Holy crap. We're an hour into setting up, and we haven't even recorded a second yet."

That sort of thing still happens occasionally. I have to be clear with the kids about when I'm doing something "uninterruptable," but they still have a way of blending work life and family life on a regular basis. It does kind of slow down my work a little bit, but I've just learned to make it a part of who I am and what I do. Business is business, but you have to be willing to let a little kid steal the show from time to time.

WHEN YOU'RE IN business, the madness is also a steady state. It's staying up late to get things done after the kids go to bed. It's tiring yourself out making progress on lots of little things but not the big, important ones you should be working on. It's realizing that traveling to speak at a two-day conference doesn't take only two days of your life and energy, but more like a week's worth once you factor in preparation and recovery. It's trying to figure out how to parse out your increasingly scarce attention to all of the people, tasks, projects, and ideas that demand it. It's having so much to do—whether you want to do it or not—and only so much time in the day to do it.

And the madness never goes away; it only changes form. It's always going to be there, and I've come to expect it and welcome it whenever I try new things. But the madness is not a bad thing. It's just a by-product of moving forward. You're never going to know if things are going to work out. You're never going to know the right way to do things, except through experience. One thing I've learned is that life is 20 percent what happens to you and 80 percent how you react to it. That's why I've come to appreciate it when things are a little messy, because it helps me understand that I can always do better, and to see where there's room for growth and improvement.

The madness is rarely awesome, but it's never the worst thing in the world, either. Sometimes the madness is even fun. Most importantly, it can teach you many, many things: to be your unique, authentic self, to not take things personally, to appreciate your family, to embrace serendipity, and to enjoy the chaos whenever and however you can. So when the madness arrives, in whatever form, see it as a golden opportunity to let go and learn something new that will carry you onward and upward.

THE MACHINE

"Compared to the early days, it's a whole different ballgame."

Pat Flynn

IN THE BEGINNING, SOMETHING FUNNY HAP-PENS TO ALMOST EVERY NEW ENTREPRE-NEUR.

You hear so much talk about "escaping the nine-to-five." But then, once you've escaped the nine-to-five, you find yourself just going along, hacking it, working from home and fitting things in when you can.

With all this newfound freedom, things get out of whack, because you don't have any structure.

Over time, I've realized you absolutely need that structure. You need systems. You need things in place to organize your work or nothing important will get done. As I talked about in previous chapters, there were points in my journey that made it clear I needed to create more structure and be more strategic. One of them was seeing Michael Hyatt's team in action at the first Platform Conference. Having my kids was another huge factor in shifting my priorities and driving me to become smarter and more efficient about everything.

For a while, I was doing everything on my own, because that's what I knew. Before I started my own business, I had never led a team. I was just getting started in the architecture field right before I was let go, so I never got to experience what it was like to build a team, empower others, or be a leader. I realized that I needed help if I wanted to grow and get to where I wanted to be. I couldn't do it all myself.

When I started out, I was just a scrappy entrepreneur. I'd built this Frankenstein monster of a business, this amazing thing that had come to life, but it was actually just a bunch of pieces stuck together that I was adding to as I went along. I needed to get smarter about the way that monster was put together. I needed to turn the monster into a machine.

• • • • •

I WROTE THE first edition of *Let Go* by myself, but I knew it needed more polish before it was ready to launch. So in 2013, I hired Matt Gartland to edit the book. I really liked working with him and loved what he did with the first edition. After we launched the ebook version of *Let Go*, Matt came to me with some bigger ideas for what we could do with the book, and we decided to work together to launch the book on the Snippet app.

The Snippet launch of *Let Go* was a big success, and it went on to become the all-time top rated and most downloaded book on the app. But sadly, shortly after the book came out, the company decided to shift gears and focus away from publishing books.

Even though my gamble with publishing my book on a new platform didn't pay off, Matt's work coordinating everything, from design to implementation, impressed me. It was all really smooth, and I could see that Matt knew and cared about what he was doing. Matt told me that he enjoyed the work I was doing and was inspired by it. It was clearly a good fit, so we decided to chat more to see how we could continue to work together. Team Flynn was born.

In one of my early conversations with Matt, after we started formally working together, he asked me an innocuous-sounding question:

"So, Pat, what are your goals for next year?"

All I could think to say? "Oh, I just want to sell more products."

Come on, Pat. You can't take action based on that. You might have an idea of where you want to go, but you won't know exactly what to do next, how to identify all the necessary tasks and delegate them, if you only get as far as, "I just want to sell more products." You have to dig deeper. You have to crunch some numbers.

For a long time I'd thought, "How can you really predict what's going to happen?" Well, you can't—but you can still set goals and plans, and take certain actions based on those plans. You can't predict the future, but you can create it. The better you define what you want to create, the easier it'll be to work backward from that and understand what actions you need to take to get there.

So Matt offered to work with me to set concrete goals for the business; he helped me plant the "planning" seed that would later sprout. With Matt's help, I started forecasting, creating budgets, and building concrete plans for the future of the business.

Shortly after that, Matt hired Mindy to help out with our ongoing work, and that's when things started to take off. In 2014, I heard about a guy named John Lee Dumas who was coming out with a new podcast. I wanted to help him out, so I offered to be the very first interviewee on his show. When I first met with John to talk about the podcast, he told me his plan was to do an interview seven days a week.

I thought he was crazy. I said to myself, "There's no way he could do that. It takes me hours and hours and hours to do one episode by myself. How is he going to manage seven per week?" But he did it, and he's been doing it ever since.

Shortly after he launched his podcast, *Entrepreneurs on Fire*, John was living in San Diego, so I took him out to Starbucks to catch up. At the time, I had one podcast, the *Smart Passive Income* podcast. At the end of each episode, I had started experimenting with a segment called *AskPat*, in which I answered business questions people sent me.

Although my audience seemed to be enjoying the tweak to the format, it made the show long, and it also changed its vibe in a way I didn't love. So I stopped doing this extra segment at the end of each episode, but it still seemed like a loss to no longer have it. I wanted to bring it back, but I didn't have an idea of how that might work.

I sat with John at Starbucks and asked him, "Dude, how do you do what you do? Because you are like a machine."

He told me, "Pat, a couple things. One, I batch-record my episodes." Essentially, he would spend one day a week recording seven or eight back-to-back to back interviews that would cover the whole week. This helped him established a mindset for that day as interview day, so he could just crank them all out.

"That makes sense," I said, "but you still have to put it all together."

He said, "Oh, I have my VA [virtual assistant] help me put all the episodes together."

Before that point, I had been doing most of my podcast production work myself. This included recording the podcast, editing it, tagging it with the right metadata, uploading it to the host, crafting the accompanying blog post, and creating the graphics for the podcast and all of the social media messaging. Phew. I hadn't even thought about how I could lean on my team and create a super-efficient process—a minimachine—that would let me do more with less effort.

But in talking to John, all of a sudden, it clicked.

"Dude," I said to him, "what if I used a similar approach to yours and made *AskPat* a separate podcast?"

He said, "That'd be awesome. Do it. Batch it, and make it easy for yourself by having your team help out."

I'd never had anyone else touch my podcast before, but I knew that this was the way I was going to make it work. So Matt, Mindy, and I put our heads together and came up with a process to produce each episode in a smart, efficient way, one that didn't involve me doing all the work. In 2014, we launched *AskPat* as its very own podcast.

From that point on, things started to really speed up. And as we worked together on more and more initiatives, it became apparent to me that Matt and Mindy were looking out for the brand in ways I hadn't anticipated. They were starting to take it under their wing, as something they were responsible for, too. They would fix things without asking, and bring up new ideas I hadn't considered.

That? That's what you want your growing team to look like.

· · · · ·

AS OF MID-2017, we're now approaching episode 1,000 of *AskPat*. And over that period, the team—the machine—has come a long way.

Staying with the analogy, there are two important things a machine needs to stay running in good condition: *fuel* and *oil*. When it comes to running a business, I like to think of the *fuel* as the *planning*. It's what keeps us moving, keeps us motivated; it keeps the engine running. It adds energy to the system, by forcing us to continually look forward, working toward something, instead of losing steam thinking about what we should be doing next.

And the *oil* is our systems and procedures. Everything we do now has a specific protocol, whether it's a process, or a set of roles and responsibilities for a given project, or how we run our meetings. These standard operating procedures (SOPs) help things run smoothly. Without them, there would be confusion and inefficiency, and the machine would eventually grind to a halt.

Over time, our team has come up with a system that provides both the fuel and the oil that keeps the machine chugging along smoothly—and a central part of that system is our regular meetings, from the ones that happen once a week to those that take place just once a year.

The first of those meetings is our biweekly sprint review meeting. Our team works on a two-week sprint schedule. We first review what we've accomplished over the previous two weeks, presenting and discussing everything the team has completed or made progress on. This includes ongoing items like blog posts and podcast episodes, as well as one-off projects or campaigns. Then we spend the second half of the meeting planning what we're going to accomplish in the next two weeks. We'll look at each new or ongoing project, extrapolate the project into tasks, determine how many sprints it'll require to complete, then decide exactly what tasks will be completed in the next sprint. Then those tasks get delegated. This exercise also helps us understand if each project is even feasible within a given time frame, or if we need to push it back based on all the other projects we have, as well as the team's availability.

Then, every other week, I have a mid-sprint review meeting with Janna, our editorial director. It's a chance for us to catch up and discuss any new ideas or things we could be doing better editorially. It's also a chance for Janna to crack the whip to make sure that I get my editorial tasks done—and to be honest, sometimes that accountability is helpful. I don't like the feeling of letting somebody down by not upholding my end of the bargain, and having this regular meeting helps keep me on task.

Roughly once a quarter, our leadership team—Matt, Janna, and I—meets and discusses the upcoming quarterly editorial and business plan. We look at everything we're going to be launching in the next quarter, like new products, courses, and affiliate promotions. We also come up with a theme for each month for the Smart Passive Income blog and podcast, which provides a baseline for all of that month's content. Then the well-oiled machine kicks into gear: the team reaches out to podcast guests to schedule interviews, and starts planning out the details of all the blog posts for the following quarter.

We also have an annual review, where we look at the whole year and plan things out. We evaluate ongoing projects, and discuss new ideas we can add to the mix to keep things exciting. We also review how we

did in the previous year. Then we'll look forward to what we want to do in the next year, and make some projections. In the annual meetings, we also do an exercise called "stop, start, continue." This involves asking ourselves, What are some things we're doing right now that aren't working? What are some new things we can put in place to improve the business? And what are the things that are working, and that we should stick with?

Finally, Matt and I have a leadership meeting every Monday, where we talk about how things are going on a higher level and just catch up with each other. This helps us get on the same page in terms of what the team's doing and how projects are progressing.

For a while, I was kind of taking it day by day, and not really thinking more than two weeks ahead of time. Now, thanks to Matt and the team and processes he's helped me create, we're planning one, two, even three years out. We're analyzing every aspect of the business. We're looking at all of the different sources of income and how they're performing. We're setting revenue goals, and working backward from those goals to figure out what we need to do each month to achieve them. This structure provides us a framework to think big about great ways to continue to serve our audience, whether it's through new events, products, or other services. Compared to the early days, it's a whole different ballgame.

. . . . .

GRADUALLY, MATT BROUGHT several more people onto the team, including a designer, Dusty; a developer, Jonathan; and an editorial director, Janna. And Team Flynn continues to grow.

Before Janna came on board in 2015, even though I had started batching and delegating certain aspects of the business, like the *AskPat* podcast, I was still treating my blog and the *Smart Passive Income* podcast like I did in the early days—just writing it on the fly without planning ahead. I would aim to publish every Monday, but I didn't always make it. I always felt behind, felt pressured. Whenever I did get an article out on time, the moment I published it I'd think, "Okay, I've got to think of something to do for next week now." I never had a chance to enjoy the marketing and promotional aspect of things.

I was stuck in a loop of stress and production, of constantly wondering, "What's next?" It was only after Janna came on board that we nailed down an editorial calendar and started actually planning ahead when it came to a content schedule across all the different platforms. We'd add things to the calendar far in advance, then work backward to determine when all the pieces needed to be accomplished.

Setting up this system has made me realize something huge: how valuable it can be *to not have to think about everything*. It's driven my belief that you start the day with a certain amount of "thinking juice" in your tank, an idea I picked up from best-selling author and podcaster Tim Ferriss. As you go through the day making decisions, you use up that juice. Big decisions take up more juice than smaller ones. And once you've used up all your juice, you're going to start making bad decisions. You're also going to be exhausted. Knowing this has influenced me to make some big changes to my individual work and creative process. That's why I wake up and do as much work as I can in the mornings, because at night my tank is usually empty and I just don't have the creativity or energy to make smart decisions.

This approach works well for me in conjunction with our team's advance planning when it comes to content creation. As I mentioned, our team meets each quarter to plan out all of our content for the year. Then every Monday morning, I go into our content planning tool, CoSchedule, open up the post that I'm supposed to write, and I write it. I already know exactly what to write about, because we've already talked about it, and the team has even created a skeleton version of the article I can build on. I don't ever have to look at a blank screen anymore and wonder, "What am I going to write next?"

The natural outgrowth of this is that, as the team has grown and evolved, I've become more open to letting other people bring their own specialties and superpowers into the mix. I've let go of certain roles and responsibilities I used to hoard for myself—and more importantly, I've let go of the idea that I have to do everything myself or that I know everything, because I don't.

One thing I've begun to let go of is the writing. In the beginning, I wrote all of the content myself. I was worried that if I were to let others write for me, it wouldn't be authentic. But now, we use interviews and transcripts to create some of our blog content, emails, and tutorials. The content still originates from me, but it's produced in a more efficient way through recording my thoughts and then having a writer on our team, Nōn, ghostwrite it using transcripts of those recordings.

The writing process was tough to let go of initially, but the results have been pretty awesome. Along the same lines, I've let go of the editorial calendar a little bit in terms of coming up with ideas. It's more of a group effort now. I'm still very particular about what gets approved and ultimately published—but I've also let go of the idea that I have to make all those decisions myself. I've learned to trust my team to make the right calls, and to keep the brand and the value we provide in the forefront when it comes to our content.

I've also learned to let go of individually answering every single question from my audience. I still handle many of those questions myself, but I've also begun to let Jessica, my executive assistant, answer questions on my behalf. It's another thing that took me a while to get over, but it's turned out to be really helpful, because people can get their questions answered much more quickly than they did when I was swamped. As a result, I've also come to understand that I don't always have to respond as quickly as I thought I did. You have a little bit of time before people expect a reply, so waiting twenty-four or even forty-eight hours before responding, unless it's super urgent, is not a bad thing. People will still will be grateful for a reply.

I've also let go of several other things I used to do myself: editing the podcasts, as well as some of the design work. Both of those were also tough for me to let go; I love design work, especially because Photoshop is the biggest skill I took with me into the business world from my architecture career.

At a strategic level, I've come to realize that letting go so that others can contribute can bring incredible perspectives that I couldn't provide myself. A lot of the strategic insight that drives the business now often comes from the rest of the team. I'll usually take those ideas and reshape them with my own twist, but the team does a great job of understanding what works and how I would normally think about things anyway.

And when I have a new idea I want to explore—like a product or service or piece of content—I'll turn to Matt as the liaison between me and the rest of the team to make that idea happen. When I have an idea, I'll share it with Matt, we'll talk it through so he understands it, then he'll take it to the team to determine what needs to happen to get it done—in terms of time, people, and other resources. Matt will also inevitably come up with a whole bunch of other considerations that hadn't crossed my mind. I let him run with it, because that's what he's great at, and in the meanwhile I'm freed up to be creative and continue to think big about new products and offerings.

Now, there are also things in my business that I'm *not* ready to let go of, and probably never will. One thing that I won't let go of is everything that goes into my speaking engagements and presentations. This is something I know I *could* let go of, and that I know other people have let go of, but for me, presentation is performance, and it's very personal. Even when it involves prepared slides, I have my own particular way of performing on stage. This involves the content on the slides, to the choreography, to the timing, and many other aspects that go into presenting to a large audience, and it's important to me to be in control of how it all works together. I have a particular style, and even though I know I could save time by having somebody else develop my slides, for instance, because it's a live performance, there's simply a lot more at stake and I want to stay in control of the whole thing.

That's part of why I charge a premium to speak on stage, because I always try to be creative and inject myself into it, to think outside the box and deliver incredible value to the audience. As an example, for the opener to my keynote speech at the 2015 NMX conference, I recreated a scene from my favorite movie, *Back to the Future*—with a real DeLorean in it. Of course, I had a production crew help me film that short movie, but it was all my idea, my slides, my reaching out to the person who rented me the DeLorean. That performance was pretty much me, and having control to express myself like that is not something I'm ready to give up anytime soon.

· · · · ·

ALONG THE WAY, I've learned that in order to grow as a leader, you have to be grateful; you need to receive help, and receive it well. A lot of the time, your team is going to be able to contribute amazing things to your business. You have to be willing to accept that help, and to realize that your team members often know more than you do about the things that will build the brand and help you succeed.

That said, building a great team—attracting and hiring the right people, fostering a healthy work environment, and appreciating your team in way that makes them want to do good work for you—is not easy. It means aligning yourself with people who appreciate your mission, and who will contribute to that mission in their own special way, with their own special superpowers. This is no small task.

In that sense, I've been blessed to have the team I do. Creating the right culture requires great leadership, and I attribute much of that leadership to Matt, because it's through him and his agency, Winning Edits, that my team has been built. After Matt and I found alignment on the vision and mission of my business, he went out and found the right people to execute on that mission. He's done an amazing job building the team, one that lines up with the values I prize—of serving others first, of being open and honest—while keeping things fun and open to experimentation. Ours is a team in which people feel safe sharing ideas and suggestions to better the brand and better serve our audience.

One other challenging thing about building a great team, a great machine, is that it costs money. It's tough, and I know a lot of people struggle with it. They want to build a team, and they know they should, but they don't have the money to do it—or they don't think they do. But if this describes you, all you need to ask yourself is this: Have you *really* crunched the numbers? How much time are you losing by doing everything yourself? And what opportunities are you forgoing by not investing in a team?

At first, it was a struggle for me to see that line item in my income report creep up into the five-figure range; it was new, and a little scary. But now that I've essentially cloned myself six or seven times over, I can get a whole lot more done, and more importantly, help and serve even more people. I've never spent more money on anything in my entire life than my team, but I've also never made as much money, or as much of a difference for my audience, as I have since this team was put in place. Those five figures have been worth every penny.

THE METHODS: MONEY

"You first need to understand the market you're getting into, and what they're looking for.

Pat Flynn

OVER THE COURSE OF MY JOURNEY, I'VE BUILT SEVERAL MINI BUSINESSES—

sources of income ranging from advertising to ebooks to affiliate revenue to coaching and speaking.

As you may know, I believe strongly in diversifying income sources, for a couple of reasons. First, if any one of my current businesses or income streams were to disappear tomorrow, I'd still have a generous income from the others streams to provide for my family. Plus, I know that even if everything were to disappear tomorrow, I have the skills and experience at creating a lot of different income streams to quickly bounce back and succeed again.

When it comes to internet business, change is a constant. Diversifying your income sources means responding and adapting to that change—creating new forms of income when new opportunities arise, and having the flexibility to let go of ones that might have been viable once but aren't anymore. My aim in this chapter is to give you a snapshot of the different ways I've generated income online as well as talk about the one thing you have to do before you try various methods for generating your own income. (I'll give you a hint—it has to do with your audience.)

As you learned in the first part of *Let Go*, GreenExamAcademy.com was my first foray into the online business world. In fact, the very first money I made online was the $1.08 that hit my Google AdSense account from an ad on GreenExamAcademy.com. It was a tiny sum, but it was worth a million times more in inspiration. When I saw that money hit my account, I thought, "Holy crap. I can do this. Let's see what else I can do."

As you also learned in the first part of *Let Go*, thanks to my mastermind group and the advice of Jeremy Frandsen of *Internet Business Mastery*, I got the idea to turn the content on GreenExamAcademy.com into an ebook and sell it on the site. That ebook was a big success, and before long it was drawing much more income than the site advertisements. Although advertising had given me a jump-start, the ebook sales kicked things into high gear: there was a lot more profit, and even more than that, there was the pride factor. I was selling my own stuff, on my own site, rather than sending someone off the site to purchase someone else's product or service.

A couple months after I launched the ebook, I released an audio version, which did really well too. GreenExamAcademy.com also gave me my first taste of affiliate marketing—selling another product that was not my own and generate a commission from the sale of that product. Once GreenExamAcademy.com had been up and running for a while and my ebook had started selling well, I connected with GreenExam Prep.com (now gbes.com), the company that makes practice exams I used to help me pass the LEED exam, first to advertise on the site, then as an affiliate.

My next venture was SmartPassiveIncome.com, which has become the centerpiece of my brand and the hub for my business. Surprisingly,

I didn't actually make money from this site in the first year. It was just a place for me to keep track of what I was doing, what I was learning, how I was progressing, and how much money I was making, so that I could inspire others. But soon, people started asking me things like, "What tool did you use to do *X*?" and "How did you build your website?" It made me realize I had an opportunity to build more affiliate relationships by recommending to my audience the products I'd used myself, in exchange for a commission.

Affiliate marketing on SmartPassiveIncome.com quickly became my central revenue source, and I've made millions of dollars by recommending other people's products, services, and tools. But I've learned a lot along the way, and there are rules to doing affiliate marketing the right way. It's easy to do, but hard to do well. There's a particular danger with affiliate marketing, because if you do it the wrong way by recommending something that's not going to truly help your audience, you risk losing their trust. If I recommend a product that doesn't work well, they're not going to like that product, and they're also less likely to trust me. The key is to make sure it's a product that you've used yourself, one that you understand well. So, I always make sure I know exactly what I'm getting myself into in terms of affiliate marketing.

I've also generated income through niche sites—and perhaps the biggest one was SecurityGuardTrainingHQ.com, which I created in 2010 as a way to provide information for people looking to start a career in the security guard industry. This site came about as a result of a challenge by a friend to build a niche site from scratch and duel it against one he was creating. I did a ton of research on the requirements of becoming a security guard in every state in the United States, then compiled all that information on the site. It was a good niche to choose, and my hard work and research paid off. I was able to get the site to rank number one in a Google search in seventy-three days and start generating a few hundred dollars a month through advertising. That eventually grew to a few thousand dollars per month, and continues to provide that same level of income today.

Later on, I ran affiliate partnerships on the site, and added a job board. The site has consistently generated an income since it was launched. The best part is that I put zero hours into it now, because it already has the information it needs to serve its target audience.

I conducted a similar experiment in 2013 with FoodTruckr.com. I did my own keyword research and talked to food truck owners to find a hole in the market, then created a solution. I went back to the GreenExam Academy.com model of learning all about a process—in this case, starting and running a food truck—and then crafting that information into an ebook package I could sell on the site. I co-own FoodTruckr.com now, as a 50–50 partnership with another company that helps with the content and the marketing. It's still making a few thousand dollars a month through ebook sales.

In that same year, I decided to expand how I was using ebooks as a revenue source. Instead of selling them on my site like I did with the GreenExamAcademy.com and FoodTruckr.com ebooks, I wanted to think bigger and write an ebook that could reach a bigger audience via Amazon. That's how the first edition of *Let Go* came about. My next book after that, *Will It Fly?*, which was my first business book, came out in 2016. *Will It Fly?* has generated income through ebook and audiobook sales. I also created a free companion course for the ebook, which is a great way to serve my audience and get people to sign up for my email list. The audiobook sales are continuing to go strong, and actually outpacing sales of the ebook.

Podcast sponsorship is another revenue-generating method I started implementing in 2014. Initially, I didn't want sponsors on my show because I wanted to keep the show clean. However, I realized that there was an opportunity to recommend products and companies that could be helpful to my audience—things I would recommend to them anyway—and that could generate a little income as well. With the growth of the podcast, I've been able to generate anywhere between $2,500 and $5,000 per sixty-second spot, per episode, which is pretty fantastic.

In addition to that, in 2015 my good friend Chris Ducker and I created a brand called 1-Day Business Breakthrough. We had been looking for a way to work together, so we decided to hold a one-day mastermind event in San Diego. So far, we have hosted four of these events, and at each event twenty-five people would pay to come and hang out with us for a day. We offered each attendee a ten- to fifteen-minute "hot seat," in which they would share their business story, then we would break their businesses down and build them back up again. Each experience was incredibly fulfilling, and it culminated in our final event in April 2016, a fifty-person mastermind event that was streamed live. Chris lives in the Philippines, so it's challenging to get together to host these kinds of events more often. But for now, we're keeping the momentum going with our *1-Day Business Breakthrough* podcast, at 1DayBB.com.

I've also been generating income through coaching and speaking. I meet with a couple of coaching clients regularly, and they pay me a retainer to offer them advice as needed. In 2011, I started speaking on stage for free, but over time, as demand has increased, I've become more confident charging a healthy sum for that time. I've spoken around the world, and it continues to be one of my favorite things to do. I make sure to put a lot of effort and resources into each of my presentations so that they're memorable and valuable to everyone who attends.

Coaching and speaking are two income-generating tracks that have emerged as I've grown my authority in the online business space. In a similar way, in the past few years I've also been generating income through advisorship. I'm an advisor for LeadPages, SamCart, Teachable, and ConvertKit. With each of those companies, I also have an affiliate relationship.

Software products are yet another source of income. The Smart Podcast Player, a WordPress–based podcast player plugin that serves both podcasters and podcast listeners, was the first truly successful software product I've built. Although building and maintaining software is a big challenge, it's also very rewarding when you create something that can help people save time and money and improve their own businesses.

There are other revenue-generating methods that I'm trying to embrace, and one is online courses. On SmartPassiveIncome.com, online courses weren't a part of my offerings at first. But once I realized how online learning programs were helping me personally, I started to come around to the idea of creating my own. I noticed that even though I could potentially find a lot of the information I needed online for free, having that knowledge packaged conveniently in one place where I had to pay for it, and thus would have skin in the game, was valuable. Online courses have been huge for me and my development, and I've started building and offering a couple of my own courses. You can check out the current lineup at courses.smartpassiveincome.com. And there are more coming!

· · · · ·

OF COURSE, IT would be impossible to only add new revenue sources and not thoughtfully let go of others. Change is a constant, remember, especially online.

In 2009, I started an iPhone app company with my high school friend Quoc. We got the crazy idea to do this one day while we were playing golf, after reading an article about an app called iFart that had raked in over a million dollars the Christmas after it was launched. And yes, all it did was make fart noises. It blew our minds that this was even possible, so we thought, "Let's figure this thing out and see what we can do ourselves."

That business, while it lasted, was a lot of fun. We did very well, and ended up grossing over a million dollars from the apps we created. Plus, it was interesting to work with other developers around the world to create silly apps. One of our apps was called BabyMaker, and it was one of the first apps that let you take a picture of two people and combine their faces in a humorous way to create an image of what their baby might look like. Another app, our highest-grossing free app with advertisements, was called Traffic Light Changer; it was literally just a button that changed color after a few seconds from red to green, which you could use to fool your friends when you pulled up to a traffic light. Obviously, it didn't *actually* do that. All it did was sync up with the actual traffic light to create the illusion that you were controlling when the light changed but it still fooled enough people that the app took off, even though the whole idea was pretty ridiculous.

By 2015, we were still making a couple thousand dollars in residual income through the free apps and advertising, and some of the paid apps. But, over time, as I got busier with Smart Passive Income, and Quoc began working on other projects, the app business became a lower priority for both of us. More than that, as SPI grew, I was becoming more and more careful about the products and services I associated myself with. The apps we created were fun and silly, but they didn't clear the crucial bar of quality and usefulness for me. There was also simply more competition. When we started, it was a lot easier to make a splash with a silly app, because there weren't as many apps out there. But, of course, over time, more and more high-quality, sophisticated apps arrived and started out-performing ours. So in 2015, we decided to shut the company down.

Another revenue source I've largely broken away from is advertising. Now that I have a lot to offer within my own brand, I want to keep people in my ecosystem, so I'm rarely directly advertising other people's products on my site. That's not to say I never consider advertising opportunities—as I already mentioned, I still have sponsors and advertisers on my podcast occasionally—but these days, I'm much more selective. Any product I might advertise on my site has to be something I truly care about, that I know will be useful for my audience. The closest I typically come to advertising these days is doing joint venture launches a few times a year to help promote products made by people I know and trust—products that are in alignment with my brand, that I don't offer myself, and that will be helpful for my audience.

There's also niche sites. For a while, these were a focal point for me, but I've since moved away from them. Niche sites are traditionally small sites that contain a finite amount of focused information on a particular topic. A few years ago, niche sites started to take off, and a lot of people were producing sites for different focus areas in a very cookie-cutter, machine-like way. And for a little while, I was one of them. I built a number of niche sites for people who were looking for wedding invitations, or for people who were looking for trumpets.

But it didn't take long before I realized that my heart just wasn't in it. Although the sites I made were actually helping people, a lot of other people were making niche sites that weren't actually aimed at serving an audience, but simply taking advantage of algorithms and black hat strategies to draw visitors for ad revenue. That sort of approach just didn't sit right with me, and it wasn't something I wanted to be associated with, so I gradually let the niche site strategy go by the wayside.

In 2011, I actually came very close to promoting a course meant to help people create their own niche sites in a replicable way. I had built out the entire course, but right before I sent out the emails and hit *publish* on the course—even though all the videos were done and everything was ready to launch—I suddenly realized it wasn't something that would help me sleep better at night. Although I had poured hundreds of hours into this online course, and it was set to potentially make serious money, I just felt it wasn't in alignment with where I wanted to go, and who I wanted to become. It wasn't the legacy I wanted to leave for myself in this world. I realized that instead of teaching people to create repetitive little niche sites that wouldn't provide lasting value, I could help them think bigger and create more authoritative sites with true care behind them, ones that would stick around and help people over the long term.

. . . . .

SO WHERE DO you start if you want to build your own passive income business? First, although people see me as the passive income guy, I want to make it clear that there's no such thing as 100 percent passive income. Even with traditional passive income such as real estate and market investing, you still have to manage and keep track of things—and it's the same with online passive income.

The nice thing about building online income streams is that by putting in the work ahead of time, you can build a foundation so that you don't have to continue trading your time for money forever. As I say in my podcasts, you're investing your time up front so you can reap the benefits later. However, getting to that point will take you time, hard work—and some money too. In order to build a sustainable passive income stream, you have to start by being *really* active.

I've shared a number of different revenue-generating methods in this chapter, so which one is best for you to start with? My answer might surprise you: I actually suggest ignoring the whole method question entirely at first. Instead, find an audience you truly want to serve, identify their needs, then find the solutions and method(s) that will best serve those needs. You first need to understand the market you're getting into, and what they're looking for. Then, through lots of discovery—surveys, conversations—you can begin to identify that audience's biggest pain points and problems. Only then can you think about creating solutions to address those pain points, and methods to deliver those solutions.

With GreenExamAcademy.com, I had it a little easy. First of all, when I started out, I *was* my own target audience. I was scratching my own itch. In fact, that's how several of my own solutions have come about—by helping myself first, then realizing that other people had the same issue. GreenExamAcademy.com was built to keep track of my own study notes, and then it organically became a resource for others too. The Smart Podcast Player was originally built to serve my own podcast, and other people happened to have the same need. Even SmartPassive Income.com started this way: In the beginning, I used it to learn about the space of my business, to keep track of my income over time, and to see how I could learn and improve along the way. But by sharing that process and those findings openly on the site, other people were drawn in, and eventually I was able to build up trust as an authority in that space.

So how should you get started? First, realize that the *methods* themselves are secondary to the *purpose*. There are ways to make money tomorrow, but are they going to help you serve your audience down the road? Will they help you be remembered, and build your brand, or are they just going to help make you a quick buck and then be forgotten? The next big lesson is, don't focus so much on the revenue *model*. There are thousands of ways to make revenue within each niche, but you have to first align yourself, and the solutions you come up with, with a market that needs help. From there, you can start to try things out.

Now, if you're in a situation where you need to make some income in short order—if you were to hold a gun to my head and say, "Pat, tell me the quickest way to make some money!"—the very first thing I'd suggest you do is simply provide a service. Freelance. Use your skills to serve a group of people who need what you can provide. Maybe you're a writer, or a designer, or a product manager—whatever it is, there are people out there who need what you have to offer. So take the skills you have, and provide them to people who need those skills in the space you're interested in.

This can help you draw an immediate income, although it won't be passive at all. But more importantly, it will allow you to enter the space you want to be in, to get familiar with it and how it works, and to see where there might be gaps you can fill. It will also give you a chance to learn about the top players in that space and start building relationships with them. Because you never know—you may be just one relationship away from discovering something that could be pivotal for advancing your career, and your life.

THE METHODS: MASTERY

"The more I've become comfortable with the idea of failure, and appreciative of what failure can teach me, I've become less afraid of failing.

Pat Flynn

MASTERING THE ART AND SCIENCE OF ONLINE BUSINESS IS ABOUT MORE THAN SIMPLY RUNNING A BUSINESS.

It's about constantly learning, growing, improving, building relationships, and taking care of yourself. Thankfully, there are also great methods for all of these things, and I want to share with you some of the ones that have been helpful to me.

Back in early 2013, I was a content junkie. I was subscribed to a feed with about twenty podcasts and forty different blogs. Content was flowing to me in a steady stream, and throughout the day I would be constantly reading the headlines, seeing if the next item piqued my interest. When I had any downtime, I'd play the next episode or read the next post on my list. As a result, I was taking in a ton of information—and learning a few things—but I was also shooting myself in the foot. I was learning, but I wasn't being strategic about it. I wasn't necessarily learning the right things, the things that would propel me forward.

Later that year, Jeremy Frandsen, my mentor from *Internet Business Mastery*, introduced me to a concept called *just-in-time (JIT) learning*. The idea with JIT learning is to only learn about things related to the very next thing you're working on, and to treat everything else as a distraction. After hearing about JIT learning, it hit me: I had been distracting myself with all this so-called learning. How many people read tons of books and listen to podcasts but then don't take any action based on the information they've consumed? Around the time Jeremy introduced me to JIT learning, my daughter had just been born. I already knew I had to become more efficient with my time.

Shortly after that, I implemented JIT learning for myself, and it's been life-changing. I unsubscribed from all but two podcasts and stopped reading blog posts entirely. I learned quickly, though, that JIT learning comes with its own fear of missing out. I was still getting my feeds, and I was trying hard not to open them. They were so enticing! Anytime I saw an article or podcast episode, in my feed or elsewhere, I'd think, "That could be really useful!"

What I did to address this was to begin organizing and filing away any interesting-looking content that came my way. If I saw a great article about how to market on Pinterest, for instance, I wouldn't read it right away, but stash it in an Evernote folder labeled "Pinterest marketing." That way, if I ever decided it was time to learn about Pinterest marketing, all the articles on that topic would be in one place, waiting for me.

But what actually happened as a result of this new system was a little unanticipated. All those folders in Evernote? I never actually open them. They're just there to collect articles that look interesting. What this system really does is help me to be okay with *not* reading all that content. Simply knowing that I *could* read it if I wanted to or when the time is right helps me overcome the FOMO.

A lot of the time, you'll read something, then put it aside and think, "That was awesome," but you don't implement anything as a result. But now, whether it's blog content, podcasts, books, courses, and even live events, I use a JIT learning approach to help make sure that I'm consuming material that actually relates to the thing I'm working on next. It focuses my learning on things I can implement right away, so that I can connect my learning directly to action. I'm able to let go of the noise, the unnecessary information that's all around me constantly, and instead focus on cultivating knowledge and skills that actually matter in my business and my growth.

· · · · ·

IN THE FIRST part of *Let Go*, as well as in the previous chapter, I talked about the mastermind group that was formative for me back in the early days of GreenExamAcademy.com. Since 2009, I've been a member of that and one other mastermind group. Both of these groups have met weekly for more than five years—and I wouldn't be where I am without either of them.

What is a mastermind group? It's a space where people who are on similar paths can meet to to share ideas, seek accountability, and set goals publicly with a small group that can provide support, guidance, and honest feedback—and a kick in the pants when necessary.

A huge key to success for any mastermind group is structure. I've been in other mastermind groups before where there was no structure, and the groups eventually fell apart. On the other hand, both of the masterminds I'm in now are very formal. We meet via an online video conference call weekly, for one hour. For the the first ten minutes, we go round-robin and talk about a personal win from the previous week. This helps keep everyone motivated off the bat. Then, each week one person is in the "hot seat," meaning they have the floor for about forty-five minutes to talk about whatever they like. Most of the time, this involves presenting a project they're working on so they can get feedback from everyone else. Other times, it's a chance to share an emotional or psychological blocker that's preventing them from moving forward in some way.

From there, each person takes a turn offering their honest opinions and suggested actions for that person. When you're in the hot seat, getting a range of perspectives can help you look at your issues from different angles. When you're working on your own stuff, it's hard to see it from the outside, which is why coming together with like-minded people in this setting is important.

Finally, we spend the last five minutes discussing some of the big goals that we each want to accomplish in the following week. Each call is led by a moderator, which is the person who was in the hot seat the previous week. The moderator's job is to keep the conversation going, to call on people if they're not speaking up, and to keep track of time— he or she keeps everyone on track, and makes sure that the person in the hot seat gets what they need out of the meeting.

My mastermind groups have been completely vital in helping me grow my business. I can't imagine my life without them. I've learned so much from hearing about other people's successes and struggles, and the ideas and solutions people come up with in these calls. More and more, whenever I encounter challenges in my business, I can immediately relate them to conversations or situations that have come up in one of my mastermind groups.

As a result, I highly recommend everybody get involved with a mastermind group. Your mastermind can be as small as two people, or it could be much larger. I gave a presentation at Social Media Marketing World in 2015 that offered several tips for being successful with mastermind groups. You can check it out at smartpassiveincome.com/tv/mastermind-groups-are-the-secret-to-success-tips-and-presentation.

· · · · ·

MASTERMIND GROUPS AND just-in-time learning are two strategies that have been awesome for my continued growth and learning. But perhaps the one thing that continues to teach me more than anything is simply *experience*: experimenting, trying, and failing. I'm always

trying new things, and my failures have taught me an immense amount. I firmly believe I wouldn't be where I am today without them.

The more I've become comfortable with the idea of failure, and appreciative of what failure can teach me, I've become less afraid of failing. Failure ultimately allows me to reach my successes more quickly. If I were overly worried about failing, I'd stunt my progress. That's a big reason I've long thought of myself as the "Crash Test Dummy of Online Business"—because I try something that may or may not work, and then report back about it for everyone else's benefit.

When an experiment fails, I'll typically write about it. This exercise usually turns into a blog post that eventually makes its way into one of my income reports. This is part of what makes those income reports much more than just income reports. They're a way to chart the lessons I've learned along the way. When I do this kind of postmortem exercise after each business failure, I ask myself things like, "What could I have done differently?" and "What was the failure point?" That way, when I encounter a similar issue or go through a similar process again, I have some guidelines to steer me toward success.

I think it's important to do this kind of analysis anytime you experience a failure. That way, when you dust yourself off and try again, you can do so in a more intentional way, with the full benefit of your experience. When you're constantly failing and trying again, without giving yourself a chance to reflect on the *whys* of that failure, you're simply not giving yourself the best opportunity to succeed. But by spending a little time considering exactly why you failed the first time around, you'll be able to approach it a lot smarter the next time.

· · · · ·

CONSTANT LEARNING AND growing is great, but if it doesn't lead to improvements in what you're providing the world, then it's of limited value. You need to apply your mastery in service of your audience.

One of the most straightforward ways I've tried to improve what I do over the past few years is by increasing the quality of my content—particularly my blog posts and podcast episodes. When I started, I was just figuring things out as I was going along. Although I never felt like I was publishing anything substandard, I've put a lot of time, effort, and care over the years into making sure that my content stays great.

For instance, in the early days, I never actually had another person read my blog posts before they came out, but now I do. And I have a professional audio editor edit my podcast episodes. I've also studied best practices for interviewing and podcasting so that I know what works and what doesn't, and I can translate what I learn directly into the product I provide to my audience. I'm always trying to improve my craft, so I'll listen to my old episodes to understand what I'm doing right and what I can improve upon.

In the past few years, I've also upgraded the look and feel of Smart PassiveIncome.com pretty significantly. The website has gone through several enormous updates, and I've captured the history of all these changes in a blog post you can find at smartpassiveincome.com/spi-theme-design. I've made a number of behind-the-scenes improvements that have had a big impact on the quality of the site—things like upgrading my web host, and hiring somebody to help me with search engine optimization (SEO). These are things that make the experience better for my audience by making it faster and easier for people to find information on my site.

What really matters is continually asking and answering the question, "How can I better serve my audience?" I'm always open to learning about what I can do to improve. My audience has taught me so much, and I try to always stay open to their feedback, whether it's through blog comments, emails, or social media. One of the best ways to improve your business is to simply ask the audience.

Two years ago, I began a practice of reaching out to ten people in my audience each month via email, offering to get on a Skype call for ten minutes and chat about whatever they like. This has turned into a really cool exercise, because it has allowed me to connect with my audience, and understand and dissect how they feel about what I'm doing. I ask them what they need help with, and in return I get some amazing personal stories and advice from people who can influence the direction of my business.

Although I typically try to keep these conversations to ten minutes or less, sometimes they go a lot longer—and that's never been a bad thing. Some people are very honest and thorough about things I can improve, while others are grateful about certain things I've done. Both of these types of feedback are great for aligning my mindset and making sure I'm doing the right things.

These calls have been a great way for me to better connect with my audience, and in so doing, to grow and strengthen my brand. I've realized that I can come up with as many ideas as I want on my own, but unless they resonate with my audience and the problems they're having, then I'm just stabbing in the dark. This practice has helped me get to know my audience, to feel empathy for where people are in their own journey, and to better understand what I can do to help them. It keeps me inspired.

Even though I've been doing it for a couple of years, talking to people and getting feedback this way still feels new, exciting, and fun. It's been a fantastic and rewarding exercise, and it's something I challenge any entrepreneur to do for themselves, their brand, and their audience too.

·   ·   ·   ·   ·

HOWEVER BIG MY brand becomes, that element of personal connection—of being able to hop on Skype for ten minutes with someone to learn how I can better serve them—is something I'll never be willing to let go of. This stems from the recognition that probably the most important thing in helping me get to where I am has been my relationships.

Every big thing that's happened in my business, every step that's propelled me forward, has come about as a result of the relationships I've built. I sometimes think, if I could go back in time and change one thing or try something different, what would it be? What guidance would I give my younger self? One thing I would definitely tell younger Pat is, stop worrying so much about what people might think about you, and just try to meet and befriend as many people as possible. Because you're only one relationship away from something amazing happening that will help you move forward.

You cannot do this alone. And so, developing strategies for building your relationships and your network is crucial. One of the biggest ways I've built my own network is through serving others first. So, if there's someone I want to connect with, I'll try to help them out in some way. This is how Derek Halpern of Social Triggers built his business. He reached out to me, and provided value for me by telling me how I could better collect email addresses on my website. I implemented what he said, and it worked, and I'm forever grateful. If you provide value first, and do it in a genuine way, without asking for anything in return, a lot of the time that return just comes back to you naturally. You can do this by promoting and sharing other people's stuff, or just by rooting them on.

Social media, and especially Twitter, has been great for making connections and starting conversations. Another top relationship builder for me has been my podcast. I've found that sometimes, if you reach out to somebody and ask if you can talk to them for forty-five minutes, they'll say no. But if you say, "Hey, can I feature you in my podcast? I'd love to share your story with my audience," They're much more likely to say yes. As a result, the podcast has become an amazing vehicle for not only providing value and content to my audience, and

I ALSO KNOW THAT THIS IS THE LIFE THAT I CHOSE, AND IT HASN'T COME ABOUT AS A RESULT OF OTHER PEOPLE TELLING ME WHAT TO DO.

helping me become a better communicator and sell more books and products, but also helping me build great connections with the people I've interviewed.

I can guarantee that I wouldn't have been able to get access to a lot of people if not for the podcast. And it's more than just getting access; it's about building relationships. I've had meals with and developed great friendships with some of my guests. That's why podcasting is such an important tool. Even if the advertising dollars weren't there, even if nobody were listening, it would still be worth doing for those relationships alone.

Finally, remember that the online world is obviously great for connecting—but one of the best ways to form the relationships that will help you grow your online business is to get offline. The mastermind groups I'm a part of now were formed as a result of meeting people in person at conferences. Conferences in particular are great places to learn, meet your fans, and connect with other influencers who could become partners and confidants. Of course, although the payoff is usually worth it, attending a conference often requires a big investment of time, energy, and money, so it's not easy to make it happen more than a few times a year. But you don't have to go to a conference to make the connections that will enrich your business and move you forward—it could be as simple as joining a coworking space, or striking up a conversation with someone in a coffee shop.

· · · · ·

STAYING SANE, MAINTAINING a work–life balance, having... fun. If you can't find a way to prioritize those things, then what's the point? A few methods have helped me maintain that balance.

A big one is my calendar. The calendar is a source of truth, and a powerful tool for organizing everything that's happening in the business, especially with all the different projects I'm juggling and all the team members involved with each of them. But it's not just the calendar itself; my executive assistant, Jessica, manages the calendar and acts as a filter for what's being asked of me versus what is actually feasible given my schedule. Her help is a huge key for maintaining my sanity, by making sure I don't say yes to too many things or let appointments overlap.

Another important practice for keeping me centered is journaling. Every morning, I use my Five-Minute Journal to think about what I'm grateful for, as well as the things I want to accomplish that day. Then, at the end of the day, I use the journal to ask myself, "What are three amazing things that happened today?" and "What's one thing that I could have done better?" This exercise has been huge for structuring my mind to think positively and being thankful for where I find myself every day.

The next practice that has helped me stay much more focused and calm is meditation. I used to think of meditation as kind of a woo-woo thing. I thought it was a little weird, to be honest. Then, I started hearing lots of entrepreneurs and others talking about how amazing meditation had been for them, in terms of clarity and keeping their mind focused. So, I decided to give it a serious try. After daily meditation for just a short period, I totally reconsidered my initial impression of this practice, because it's rapidly become an important part of my daily life.

I spend ten to fifteen minutes meditating every day, in the mornings, right after I journal. After doing it for a little while, I've seen direct results from it: my mind isn't racing in a bunch of different directions all the time like it used to, and I can stay focused on one thing for much longer. It used to be that if I got interrupted while working, it would knock me off balance, and could take twenty or thirty minutes to an hour to get back to where I was before. But now, since I started meditating, I can get back into that state of flow almost right away after getting distracted.

The final key to helping me stay creative and energized has been exercise and fitness. I've learned I need to keep my energy levels up and stay strong and focused, because if I don't, I'll start to fall behind on everything.

In the end, all these things are great tools. Tools to maintain your focus, energy, and sanity through the rigors and distractions of each day. But there's one more factor that's more important than all these strategies and methods, and that's loving what I do. At the end of the day, despite the swirl of running a huge online business, it doesn't feel like work at all. Yes, I get stressed; I would never lie about that. I get frustrated when things don't work out the way I want them to. But, I also know that this is the life that I chose, and it hasn't come about as a result of other people telling me what to do. It's been my own plan, my own path. It's fun, I love it, and I feel grateful and blessed for every moment, win or fail, because I've carved it myself.

So ask yourself, "Do I love what I do?" If you don't love what you're doing, what would it take to get you there? What can you do, starting today, to get a little closer to that point? You can start small—but start you must.

THE MOMENTUM

"As I've grown, it's become easier to imagine where my journey could take me in the future.

Pat Flynn

IN THE BEGIN-NING, I THRIVED ON MY CON-NECTION WITH MY AUDIENCE— ON BEING COMPLETELY INTERACTIVE WITH AND RESPONSIVE TO THEM.

I would answer every blog comment, every email. I tried to listen and provide them with everything they needed, both because I loved to do so and because I felt it would differentiate my brand from everyone else's out there.

But over time, as my business continued to grow, I started to lose touch. I could no longer respond to everyone as quickly as I had before. I began to feel disconnected from the people I served. At the same time, I was becoming overwhelmed with everything else in my business. I was drowning in emails, drowning in all the tasks on my to-do list. I felt like I was stuck underwater, yelling and screaming for help, but nobody could hear me.

During that dark time, I never stopped caring about my audience. But I was stuck, out of reach of the people I was trying to serve. It wasn't until I really started to adopt a CEO mindset—to lean on the team I was building and create systems and procedures that could help me get my head above the water again, that I was able to re-establish meaningful productivity and reconnect with my audience.

At first, though, I was scared of becoming a CEO, because in my head, the CEO was the person on the top floor of the building who wore a suit, and who nobody could talk to except high-level team members. I didn't want to be that kind of CEO. I wanted to be an accessible CEO, but to do it in a smart way where I wouldn't become overwhelmed again.

Thankfully, as I talked about in "The Mindset," that's not what a CEO has to be or do. Now, with my team, and the tools, processes, resources, and investments we've put in place, I'm at the point where I can be there—and stay there—for my audience again.

I'm still not able to answer and reply to every single email or every single tweet—and I probably never will—but hopefully people realize that I'm still accessible and that I care about staying in touch. My connection with my audience is fundamental to me, because through everything I've been through, they've always been there for me.

Whether it's Michal's inspiring story of recovery and triumph after a major injury, or the simple thank-you notes people send me that I post on my wall as inspiration to keep going when I get in a funk—because yes, sometimes I still do—these are the things that help me keep my head above water. But more than that, my audience inspires me to think bigger, to continually level up in terms of how I serve them. In the past few years in particular, I've started to pour a lot more resources into building the team, improving the website, adding new offerings like software and courses, and continuing to explore other solutions to serve my audience.

In the beginning, it was just me, honestly sharing the successes and roadblocks of my entrepreneurial journey via my blog. Then I took the leap to YouTube. At first, I was a scared to put myself on camera, but gradually I became more comfortable with it. That evolved into the podcast in 2010, and then speaking on stage in 2011. Now I speak all over the world, and I'm starting to put on my own live events.

At this point, I'm super focused on growing and improving by continually providing higher-level, higher-quality forms of education and connection for my audience. I recently leased a 900-square-foot office space here in San Diego about ten minutes from my home, where I'm building a video studio. It's a big investment, but I know that it's going to earn a return in many ways, not just in terms of income, but also through my ability to share more information with people at a consistently high level of quality.

I'm also building on the small workshop experiences I've created, such as the 1-Day Business Breakthrough events with Chris Ducker. Those will evolve into weekend-long intensives to share some of my most valuable strategies with people who want a higher-touch experience. They're also going to evolve into larger live events, which will hopefully be avenues for people struggling with the limiting beliefs that come up whenever they try something new, to help them push through and get squarely on the path to their next great thing.

• • • • •

AFTER ALL THIS time, my wife, my parents, and other people who know me well sometimes get asked: "What exactly does Pat do?" Often, they don't know how to reply, because I do a lot of things.

So, what do I do? Well, I serve others by building my businesses and running experiments so that others can live a fulfilled life and serve others as well. But to be honest, even though I've been on this path for almost ten years, the process of defining exactly what I do, and why, has been ongoing. And to be even more honest, sometimes the question "What exactly does Pat do?" trips me up, too.

A big milestone in that process of understanding exactly how I serve others occurred earlier this year, when I attended Pete Vargas's Advance Your Reach conference. On the first day, I went to a session with Chris

Smith. Chris uses a process called The Campfire Effect to help people understand their strengths and better define their brands. One of the things Chris emphasized to us in his session was the need to create some sort of proprietary method or "recipe" for whatever it is you offer.

After his talk, he gave us time to go through an exercise to determine the recipe for our own brands. As I started the exercise, I thought, "Oh, I've got this. This will be easy." But as I was sitting there, it wasn't coming so easily. I was writing things down. I was crossing things off. And I suddenly realized, "Wow, I haven't actually figured this out yet."

So I started brainstorming and thinking, "Okay, what do I actually teach people to do?" And what I came up with is what I call the Four Ps. Those Ps are purpose, platform, products, and passive income.

The first P, *purpose*, is about understanding why you're doing what you're doing. It's your mission. Without it, without that navigation, that destination in mind, you're going to end up going in directions that might not be right for you. It's the address you need to plug into your business's GPS, or you'll just end up driving around, losing gas.

The second P, *platform*, is about taking your mission and figuring out how you're going to share it. It's about determining, as Michael Hyatt says in his book titled (not surprisingly) *Platform*, how to be found "in this noisy world." This is what I help people do. I help them understand what platforms are available to them, who they can serve, and where they might be able to find the audience who needs to hear their message.

The third P involves asking what *product* or *products* you can create to help solve the problems of the people in your target market. This leads directly to the fourth P, *passive income*. Once you've built your products or services, whether they're online courses, physical products, software, client work, or something else, you can then figure out how to automate things, to free yourself up to focus on creating even more value for your audience elsewhere.

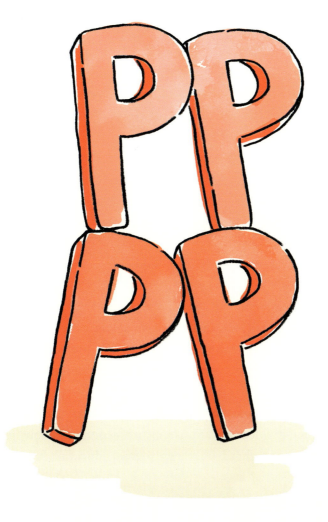

FOR A WHILE, the money coming into the business has exceeded the number of dollars my family needs to survive each month and support all the things I want to fund. With this additional income, I've started to look at how I can make an impact outside of my network—how I can help effect positive change in the world in a bigger and better way.

I volunteered for a lot of causes while I was younger, and it has always been a goal of mine to get involved in philanthropic work at a larger scale—but I didn't think it would happen by the age of thirty-three. In 2014, for my birthday, instead of asking for birthday wishes and gifts, I asked my community and audience to contribute to a campaign hosted by an organization called Pencils of Promise to help build two schools in a village in Ghana. I challenged them to raise $25,000, and promised that if they did, I would match it.

We did just that, and the experience that unfolded was incredibly exciting and eye-opening. I had rallied my community to make real change together. It showed me the power of what I had built, and the fact that I wasn't just building a business for me, or even for others who were trying to build their own businesses. I could change the lives of people well outside my usual sphere of influence.

In June 2015, I visited Ghana with Pencils of Promise to see how the money we raised was being put to use. The trip was was life-changing for me. During that visit, although the two schools the SPI community and I had helped build were already up and running, I went to a ribbon-cutting ceremony for two other schools that had recently been completed. We even helped with the construction—actually got our hands dirty—for one other school that was just getting started. It was incredibly inspiring to see education being wholeheartedly celebrated in these villages that hadn't had access to good educational facilities until that point.

My trip also brought me back down to Earth a little bit, and I realized how people in Western cultures often take what they have for granted. At the schools in Ghana, there were no playgrounds, and very few toys and equipment. These kids literally played with sticks and dirt, but they were making use of what they had, and they were so happy. During the visit, I played soccer with a bunch of kids for an hour just using trees as goalposts—and it was probably the most fun I've ever seen kids have. They were absolutely enjoying life, in a place where a lot of Westerners wouldn't even know what to do with themselves. It brought things into perspective for me when I got back home and realized how grateful I am for what I have access to.

The experience also inspired me to see what else I could do beyond my existing network and beyond my business, which is why I joined Pencils of Promise as an advisor, to help the organization and influence their direction in a positive way. Being an advisor to Pencils of Promise has also given me a chance to reach out to a lot of the amazing minds who are advisors in the philanthropic community, people who might serve as resources down the road as I try to expand my philanthropic work.

I love what Pencils of Promise has been doing in the world under the direction of their founder, Adam Braun—check out Episode 102 of the *SPI* podcast to learn how he's contributing to the world by building schools in different countries.

Another major way I want to expand my philanthropic work is closer to home, in the field of education. I have a son who's seven and a daughter who's four, and now that they're a little older and in school, I'm seeing just how broken parts of the education system are. I've seen how our educational system is falling short and failing to deliver for our kids. It's not keeping up with the times that we live in; instead of preparing kids for the real, fast-changing world, it's putting them in boxes, treating them as units on a factory assembly line. I also see how teachers aren't being adequately rewarded for the hard work that they do, and that's something that needs to change too. And so I'd like, with my influence and the resources I have, to work to make some change in that world now too.

. . . . .

AS I'VE GROWN, it's become easier to imagine where my journey could take me in the future. Five years ago, I wouldn't have guessed that I'd find myself where I am now—because back then, I just didn't know what was possible. At first, I just wanted to survive. Then, I tried to start building my business, but I had no real thought about where it should go. I was focused only on the day-to-day. I'd hit publish on a blog post then think, "Okay, well, time to think about what's happening next week." Things were going well, and income was growing, but I still wasn't thinking that far ahead.

It wasn't until my team came on board and I started to adopt a CEO mindset that I began to think a lot more about the future. Since then, it's become easier to imagine what's possible. A big reason for that is I now have more wins under my belt. I've realized that I can actually do many of the things that I think up! But at the same time, I'm also aware that I don't know exactly what'll happen, because there's so much that's bound to change in unexpected ways. Technology is constantly getting faster and better, and it's branching into entirely new areas, particularly with the arrival of virtual and augmented reality. No one truly knows what's going to happen.

But regardless of what I know or don't know about the future, if I'm only thinking a short period ahead, I won't be ready for what's to come—whatever that ends up being. One thing I've taken with me from my early days in my *Internet Business Mastery* mastermind group is the idea that in order to get big results, you have to take bold actions.

That *being reactive isn't being bold; it's just being told.*

It's the difference between being reactive and being proactive. Being reactive can be fine sometimes, because often you need to adopt and adapt to the reality that's presented to you. But being proactive means you're actually creating your future; you're aiming higher, so even if you don't end up where you hoped, at least you took a purposeful approach that will continue to guide you.

Through all of the different stages and milestones of my journey have also come a number of mentors and people who've inspired me to be proactive and aim higher. In the beginning, it was Jeremy and

Put **yourself** out there, ask for **feedback**, invite people to **share** their stories with you. You might be **surprised** how much of an **impact** you're actually **having**.

Jason from *Internet Business Mastery* and all the people they interviewed on their podcast. Then it was Tim Ferriss and Ramit Sethi. Chris Ducker fired me up to finally get some virtual help and build my staff, and Michael Hyatt encouraged me as I began to grow my team and expand their responsibilities. Amy Porterfield was a huge influence in learning how to manage my schedule and calendar for maximum efficiency. Adam Braun was a big inspiration for me in terms of how I could help others in this world who might be beyond my initial circle of reach.

Now it's Elon Musk, who is thinking and acting in ways that are inspirational to me; there seems to be no limit to what's possible to him. He built Tesla from the ground up. He wants to go to Mars. He wants to solve the traffic problem in LA by creating underground transportation. For every idea he has, every problem he wants to solve, he's already thought it through. He's already come up with most of the process and answered the questions that people might have. Although not all of his ideas are likely to pan out, he's made plans and anticipated the challenges.

More than anyone, he exemplifies thinking big, and it's the way I want to think too. Seeing his example makes me wonder, "Why can't I think like that? Why have I always had these ceilings on my goals?" So, more than anything, at this point, I've been looking to remove those ceilings, to dream even bigger than I think I can.

Part of thinking bigger and looking deeper into the future is also about understanding what I want my legacy to be. I want to be somebody who is remembered for doing business the right way, who helps others and inspires them to be transparent with their own customers, who makes them realize that they have this amazing power to create their own business that will serve its customers and make change. I want people to understand that they can't even imagine how great they might be until they actually put in the effort and start letting go of their limiting beliefs.

Sometimes, though, when you're so deep in your business, you don't see the impact that you're having or the legacy you're creating: you forget to look for it, or it's just not that easy to see. And there have been moments along the journey when I've wanted to give up—to halt the momentum—because I've been working so hard on something and not getting the results or feedback I wanted. But a lot of the time I forget a simple truth: even if what I'm doing is actually helping someone, they aren't going to tell me all the time, because they're busy putting my advice into action! They're doing exactly what I told them to do.

Thankfully, people like Michal Szafranski will pop in now and again to let you know how important your work is, and to inspire you to keep going. But if you've been working hard and feeling dejected because you're not seeing or hearing from the people you're working for, you don't have to wait around for them to come to you. Put yourself out there, ask for feedback, invite people to share their stories with you. You might be surprised how much of an impact you're actually having. Sometimes all it takes is a nudge.

. . . . .

A LOT OF PEOPLE say to me, "Oh, man. You're so lucky." And I have been lucky for the opportunities that have come my way, but I also know that I've been purposeful in making decisions to take action. My layoff was the catalyst for me to break out of my routine, look around, and see something new that I could grab ahold of and try. Even though I didn't know all the answers at the time, I sought out and got involved with people who helped me figure out what to do. I didn't know exactly how it would all turn out, but I took action and thankfully, great things happened.

Like everybody else, I like to see results. I want that momentum to pick up quickly, and to carry things along. And in a way, that momentum did gather for me relatively quickly. But it's not like my success happened overnight. A lot of things had to happen beforehand to get to a point where I could monetize and build out my business.

This goes along with something Gary Vaynerchuk said once, which is the idea of "micro hustle" and "macro patience." "Micro hustle" means working hard on all the small things that are going to move the needle for you; focusing in and perfecting each piece that's going to get you closer to your goal. Then on a macro level, you need to be patient while you wait for the results, because they may not come right away.

I love this concept, because more and more these days, people expect super-fast results. We search for things on Google, and we get the answers in fractions of a millisecond. Everything is on-demand. Everything but results. You can get easy access to opportunities, but not results.

You have to work, then wait. Put in the effort, then let go.

• • • • •

WHEN I WAS seven, I took karate classes. One day in class, we were given a new challenge: break a piece of wood with our hands. I remember thinking before we began that this couldn't be possible. How could someone break a piece of wood with their bare hands? But older students were coming in and demonstrating it. They were doing it. It just looked so cool and impossible to me; it was fascinating, but also unbelievable.

Now, that's the thing: if you don't believe something will happen, it probably never will. Thankfully, there were two things my instructors taught me that helped me believe it was possible, eventually allowing me to break my first board.

The first was to imagine punching something behind the board—to make sure that you follow through. You need to be thinking ahead of or beyond your immediate target.

The second was just as important. After they did the demonstrations, they split the students into groups of two. I was really excited to go first, so I gave my partner the board to hold.

I tried and tried, but the board wouldn't break. I tried tiger palming it. I tried kicking it. My partner was getting knocked over. The board just wasn't breaking, and I thought, "This isn't gonna work."

But the instructor saw what was happening, and he came over and said, "Hold on a sec." He turned the board 90 degrees and said, "Go." And then I was able to punch through it.

I didn't realize that, depending on how your partner holds the board, if you're punching against the grain, you're never going to break it. But if your partner holds the left and right sides of the board so that the lines in the wood are pointing up and down, it takes far less effort to break it. All it requires is a simple turn of the board; a change in position.

When it comes to taking bold action, more force is rarely what's needed, but that's where a lot of people get it wrong. They think, "Oh, I just have to work harder." It's more about thinking things through and setting them up correctly, working smarter in the here and now, so that whatever you're trying to do requires less force to achieve more action.

People love to talk about *hustle*. And hustle is great, but there's another element to it. Hustling your way to success is not only about working hard to work hard, but also working hard with a smart approach so that you can make the biggest and boldest impact. *Bold* is in the decisions you make. But *smart* is in the actions you take.

One part *bold* + one part *smart*: that's a recipe for momentum.

LET GO AND LET IN

"In order to grow, you have to let go."

Pat Flynn

IN EARLY 2017, ACTOR WILL SMITH SPOKE ONSTAGE ABOUT HIS EXPERIENCE SKYDIVING FOR THE FIRST TIME:

"**You fall out of the airplane**, and in one second, you realize that it's the most blissful experience of your life. You're flying. There's zero fear. You realize that at the point of maximum danger is minimum fear. It's bliss. Why were you scared in your bed the night before? What do you need that fear for? Everything up to the stepping out, there's actually no reason to be scared. It only just ruins your day. The best things in life are on the other side of terror. On the other side of your maximum fear are all of the best things in life."

Until you make the jump, you're surrounded by safety. But your fear is like a runaway monster, one that grows bigger and stronger the closer you get to the point of jumping. It builds and builds, then peaks right before you leave the plane.

In fact, as Smith tells the audience, when the time comes to make the dive, the instructor starts counting down to three—then pushes you on "two"—because "three" is when people reflexively grab on for dear life, terrified of launching themselves into the vast expanse of certain death sprawling out below them.

But as soon as you jump out, you're flying. Your fear vanishes the moment you let go. *It's bliss.*

The moment when things are actually the most dangerous, when you're free falling, is the moment the fear disappears. The point when you're *the least safe you could possibly be*, is when your world opens up and you can experience true joy.

The coolest things happen after you let go of your fear. After that point, what comes can be dangerous—but it's also when life gets exciting, and when fulfillment can begin. In order to experience new things, in order to get unstuck from a place you don't want to be, you have to let go, figuratively, and sometimes even physically, too.

In order to grow, you have to let go.

•   •   •   •   •

I LIVED THROUGH the scrappy entrepreneur mindset for years—the "do it yourself, just make it through the week" approach. I was able to grow and survive, but I almost drowned holding on to that mentality. But when I adopted a CEO mindset, the skies opened up.

Now, I waited until I was well into my journey before adopting this mindset. If I'd come across it earlier on, maybe I could have avoided some pitfalls. But instead of dwelling on the past and wishing I could

have done things differently, I hope instead that my experience can serve as an example to you. Knowing what I've gone through, and knowing that your future might involve similar challenges, I want to give you the chance to create the mindset and take actions that will help you avoid those challenges—or at least manage them successfully when they arise.

I want you to have the chance to become a CEO sooner than I did.

Remember, first, that the path is not always going to be pretty. In fact, it's probably going to be pretty messy. Like John Lee Dumas said once, "Every master starts as a disaster." You simply might not know what you're doing at first, and that's totally okay. But there's one thing I will tell you now, and it's the one thing a CEO does that I would recommend to anybody who's just starting out:

Get to the point where you're no longer in "What do I do next?" mode.

Get to the point where your default mode is "plan, then act" instead of "act, figure it out, act, figure it out . . ." You're always going to deal with "What do I do next?" mode to some degree; it's part of the beauty, the wide-open nature of creating your own path. But that way of thinking and doing, when it becomes ingrained in your day-to-day, can ultimately swallow your focus, your motivation, and your ability to work on the things that will get you to the next level.

When you're just starting out, bootstrapping your business, you may not have a lot of money to build a team. But at the same time, that doesn't mean you can't adopt small pieces of the CEO mindset, in terms of planning for the future and letting others take things off your plate. Even if you're at the very start of your journey, you can start to let go of the idea that you have to do everything yourself. There are tons of people and resources out there to help you, from virtual assistants to online tools to manage almost every aspect of your business.

The more you can start thinking ahead in terms of months and years, not days and weeks—planning and automating, building systems and processes to keep your head above water—the better off you'll be in the short term *and* the long run. It could be as simple as planning your content schedule more than a week in advance. Even though I have a whole team to help me with content planning and production, the basic process is one that any team or solo entrepreneur could adapt to their own business.

It will take time to get to the point where you're the CEO of your own business, but if you decide that that's where you should be headed, you'll be able to anticipate a lot of the stresses and the challenges that are going to come your way.

•   ·   •   ·   •

IN BUSINESS AND in life, things are going to break. Plans are going to go off the rails. It's going to happen, and when the madness threatens to take over, you're going to need a way to bring yourself back to center.

A big part of that for me has been meditation. My meditation practice brings me back to Earth when my mind starts to spin out of control. It helps me calm my thinking brain, so I'm better able to focus on one task at a time. It helps me check in with myself. When things don't go as planned, I'm not overwhelmed. I'm not as fazed. I still get frustrated. But I use the awareness cultivated through meditation to turn that frustration into action, instead of just complaining. And perhaps most importantly, meditation also helps me make sure I'm present when I'm with my family, so they get the best version of me.

Things will happen that you can't control, but there are still lots of things you can control, and meditation and mindfulness can help you become aware of the distinction. It's helped me become more conscious about the choices I make and how I react to things. In this way, meditation has helped me connect to the bigger picture as well, to the idea that you have the ability to create your own world and shape your reality through your choices and your actions.

Having a practice like that, one that helps you let go of the need or the urge to solve every problem by *thinking* about it, is crucial. Maybe for you, it's meditation. Or maybe it's journaling, or painting, or, I don't know, singing in the shower. Whatever it is, make it a part of your daily life, so you always have a place to go to escape the madness and find your focus again.

This brings up another important point, one that has to do with more than just meditation: *Don't knock it until you try it.*

Before I tried meditation, I had a preconceived idea that it was strange. That it wasn't for me. Now, it's one of the most important things I do every day. When it comes to self-improvement, business improvement, or *anything* improvement, there are a lot of great ideas and tools out there. On the one hand, it would be impossible—and unnecessary—to try them all. But at the same time, there are probably some ideas out there that can help you get to the next level, but you just haven't thought to try them yet. Maybe it's because they're unfamiliar, or you're afraid of them, or you just don't understand them.

So I challenge you to go exploring a little bit. Challenge your preconceived notions about what's out there that could be useful to you on your journey. Find a strategy, or a method, or a person you've rolled your eyes at before, or just never really considered, and give it a shot. Let go of your hang-ups and take a chance on something that could give you a new perspective.

Your habits and biases are going to kick in at different points along your journey. But in order to learn and grow, you have to be willing to let go of those biases, to question your assumptions about certain things, because you may be shutting yourself off from a golden opportunity to learn something new, improve a process, or even change the way you live your daily life for the better.

When you find yourself reacting negatively to some new idea or strategy, pause. Often, the things we resist are the things that could have immense value for us, but they're just not what we're accustomed to, or they represent the change and growth we're afraid to experience. Remember that there's always room for improvement, and other people and other ideas may have a lot to teach you. Be willing to let go of what you think is right or best, and let in a chance to grow.

· · · · ·

AS I TALKED about in the previous chapter, it's easy—too easy, especially in the early stages—to beat yourself up over the fact that you're not seeing the results you want. You probably remember the anxiety I experienced after putting my first ebook up for sale on the homepage of the GreenExamAcademy.com website. The morning after launching the ebook, I was sitting at my computer at work, half-checked out because I'd already been notified I was being let go from my job. Every few minutes, I was feverishly checking my sales counts, erupting in excitement whenever another book sold, and growing anxious when there was no movement.

I've grown a lot since that day. Today, looking back on that experience, I like to think I wouldn't find myself in that same state again. I can smile at the thought of young Pat, sitting, sweating at his desk, waiting anxiously for that next *Ding*! Back then, I'd gotten the "micro hustle" part down. It was the "macro patience" that I still needed to work on.

A lot of people beat themselves up over the fact that they're not getting results. Others beat themselves up because they *are* getting results—but they're just not as flashy as the results someone else may be getting. In the past nine years, there have been many more online entrepreneurs who have started businesses similar to mine, and some have ended up doing much better than me. Thanks (or not) to income reports, it's easy for a lot of us who are online entrepreneurs to compare ourselves to each other.

One of the people who came onto the scene and has grown his business to the point that he's been making more than me for a while now is John Lee Dumas. Some people might view this situation as a natural source of jealousy and tension. And in fact, a few people have even asked me, "Hey, what do you think of John Lee Dumas and his income reports? How does that make you feel that he's beating you?"

What do I think? I think, "Dude, I'm so freaking fired up for him! That's so cool!"

A lot of people feel like there's a finite amount of success in this world. That if someone else has it, you can't, especially if you're operating in the same space. But I challenge everyone to let go of that idea, and instead to operate as though there's room for everybody to succeed.

I love the fact that more people are getting into my field; it keeps me fired up to continue to do better and provide more value. If you play the comparison game, on the other hand, the only one you end up ultimately crushing is yourself. As far as I'm concerned, there's more than enough to go around—and I hope you'll embrace the same attitude about your success and the success of those around you.

It goes back to the question of whether you want to be reactive or proactive in life and in business. If you're always comparing yourself and taking action based on what someone else is doing, you're probably going to be reacting more than you're acting. So let go of comparing yourself to others, and just compare yourself to you.

At the same, I realize that people sometimes think, "Oh, Pat Flynn is special. I can't do what he's done." But hopefully, through reading my story, and realizing that I've gone through a lot of my own struggles too, maybe you'll start to see some connections between my story and yours, and even use it to begin to create something great in your own life.

There's another important lesson in there, too, and it centers on the word *relate*. *Comparing* yourself to others and *relating* to them are two different things. There's an important distinction there. As you go out into the world, as you meet people and see others finding success, try to use their success as motivation, not demotivation. Instead of endlessly comparing yourself to them, try to understand what makes them tick. Empathize, and learn from them. *Relate* to them. See that we're all on our own journey, and that we're here to help each other, not knock each other down.

It can sometimes be tough to see the success of others as inspiration rather than demoralization. We all have to be honest about the fact that although I might say, "Don't compare yourself to others," inevitably at some point, we all do that. It's in our nature. And we can allow ourselves to respond that way sometimes—but we don't have to let it guide our actions.

Instead, when you see someone else succeed, be grateful for the fact that there are opportunities out there to succeed, because that means you also have the opportunity to succeed. And then use their success as motivation to find your own path. It requires a mindset shift, and one that might feel strange at first. But over time, you'll realize that being happy and even grateful for other people's success makes the world feel bigger.

It can also be tempting to see someone more successful and want to copy them. While that's not always a bad idea, it can ultimately hold you back. I remember when I started out and I was building Smart PassiveIncome.com, I found all the websites that I liked and decided to incorporate all of their cool elements into my site. I thought, "Hey, they're successful, so maybe I can be successful doing it that way, too."

But it wasn't until I added my own spin to things and put more of myself into it that the site became something closer to what it was meant to be. It eventually become unlike anything else out there, because it was a representation of my authentic self, and that's why people ultimately gravitated toward it.

So learn all you can from others, and cheer their successes. I hope that along the way you'll find your spin, let go of the need to be anyone else, and let your authentic self inhabit whatever you do. It's the best way to be.

• • • • •

AS I WAS writing this book, my son, Keoni, started taking swimming lessons. In his first few lessons, he was afraid of the water. He never wanted to let go of the edge. (Hopefully Keoni will forgive me someday for embarrassing him twice in this book.)

In one of those early lessons, I was with him in the pool. I was standing in the water, a little ways from the edge, and Keoni was clinging to the edge, afraid to let go. I was encouraging him to swim toward me. I wasn't standing very far away from him, just a couple of strokes, but far enough that he wouldn't be able to just jump toward me; he was going to have to swim a little. I told him I would catch him—that he'd be fine, and that he just needed to let go and push off the wall.

He pushed off, and I waited a couple extra seconds—let him swim a few extra strokes—before catching him. When he reached me, he was kind of upset at me, because I hadn't caught him right after he'd let go, as I said I would.

But he'd made it. He was fine. And he didn't even realize what he'd done until I told him. He didn't register what he'd accomplished until I said, "Turn around. Look how far you are from the edge now."

"I swam that far?"

"Yeah, you don't even know how far you can swim, because you're worried you're gonna drown. But you won't."

Later that day, I talked to him a little more about what had happened in the pool. "You have this ability, Keoni," I told him. "Some of it's an ability that you already know you have, and some of it's subconscious. But you're gonna make it. You'll be fine. And, of course, I'm here for you, and I'm not going to let you drown. But I'm also going to push you a little beyond where you think you can go."

Now, there's a fine line between nudging our kids into unfamiliar territory where they can test their limits and abilities, and *Hey, let's lie to our kids so they do better*. But we need to give our kids, and ourselves, a chance to let go—of the pool's edge, of the belief that we won't make it without that support—so that we have a chance to achieve something we might not have thought was possible.

A day or two later, Keoni had another swimming lesson. I had a work call at the same time that day, so I couldn't be there in the pool with him at the start of the lesson. Instead, I arrived at the pool area in the middle of the lesson.

When I saw him, he was a totally different person. He was swimming from one side of the pool to the other, with no problem.

I couldn't believe it was him. It had taken a small—and momentarily terrifying—moment of letting go to create many bigger moments of letting go, to jump in the pool again and be confident in his abilities, to trust himself, so that he could experience the thrill of no longer being held back by his fear.

•　•　•　•　•

IN *THE WAR OF ART*, Steven Pressfield asks, "Are you paralyzed with fear? That's a good sign. Fear is good. Like self-doubt, fear is an indicator. Fear tells us what we have to do. Remember one rule of thumb: the more scared we are of a work or calling, the more sure we can be that we have to do it."

Fear is a signal that you're doing the right thing.

I spent a lot of time trying to rid myself of my fears. To let go of them entirely. But what I've realized is that a lot of the time, they're simply not going away. I still get scared whenever I'm about to go onstage, or before I'm about to try something new.

I realize now that the fear is actually a good thing. It's a sign that I'm headed in the right direction, the direction of growth. I look toward that fear now. And if I don't feel it when I'm trying something new, then it's a cue that I'm probably not going big enough.

Fear is a sign that whatever you're thinking of doing is actually worth doing, that there's probably something amazing on the other end. So let your fear be your indicator. Instead of trying to keep it at arm's length, race toward it and embrace it. The worst thing that can happen is that you fail. Of course, failure is a part of the process of growing and learning, and those failures teach you lessons. So give it a shot. Go out and fail. Do amazing things, and get to those failure points, so that you can learn, get up, and get back at it again.

There's another great quote, by Les Brown: "The graveyard is the richest place on Earth, because it is here that you will find all the hopes and dreams that were never fulfilled, the books that were never written, the songs that were never sung, the inventions that were never shared, the cures that were never discovered, all because someone was too afraid to take that first step, keep with the problem, or determined to carry out their dream."

Time will inevitably pass, and one of the worst things that could happen to you is to realize when you're older that you should have done something but didn't because you were scared. It crushes me to know that there are people out there who aren't doing the things they want to do because they've been conditioned by what they learned growing up. A lot of time, it's not their fault. We spend our early years in school being tested and graded, and we become conditioned to think that failure is the worst thing that could ever happen to us.

But it's not. It's just a false idea many of us learned from an early age, even if we didn't know it at the time and didn't start to figure it out until we *had* to start failing in order to succeed.

In order to better serve others and serve yourself, you have to internalize what's holding you back—the false beliefs or assumptions that guide your decisions and your attitudes. You need to see them for what they are, then decide if they're worth holding on to in exchange for what's potentially out there.

What's holding you back will in a lot of ways be unique to you. But there are also universal aspects of the human condition that we can point to, common patterns that we all grapple with, that we can draw out and examine and understand, so that we can either let go of them or use them to our benefit in some way.

We all have the chance to learn from each other, and I hope this book has given you a chance to learn a few things from my journey that will be helpful on yours.

So let go of the idea that there shouldn't be failure. Let go of the idea that there shouldn't be fear. Let go of judging yourself for past mistakes. Let go of these things, then let in the abundance. Let in the support of your team, of your family and friends. Let in the success of the people in your space who are carving their own path. Let in the abundance of new, unfamiliar ideas that could boost you to the next level. Let in the abundance of unexpected challenges that will mold you into who you were meant to be.

Let go, so you can let in what's on the other side of that fear.

Ready?

On the count of three, you're going to leap out of this plane.

One, two—

EXCLUSIVE LET GO BONUS VIDEO CONTENT

For the first edition of *Let Go*, I created several bonus videos that retraced some of the pivotal steps in the early part of my journey. You'll find all of this content at patflynn.com/letgo-videos.

In addition, here are links to the individual videos:

Part 1

Introduction: smartpassiveincome.com/letgoch1bonus
November 2005: smartpassiveincome.com/letgoch2bonus
June 2008: smartpassiveincome.com/letgoch5bonus
August 2008: smartpassiveincome.com/letgoch7bonus
October 2008 to January 2009: smartpassiveincome.com/letgoch10bonus
February 2009 to Mid-2009: smartpassiveincome.com/letgoch11bonus
One Last Story: smartpassiveincome.com/letgoch12bonus

Back to the Future is one of my all-time favorite movies. I love the idea of going back in time to change things that happened (a "do-over"). I think we all feel like there are things we did in our past that we wish we hadn't done, or had simply done better.

I thought it would be fun to create a little video for my younger self. Perhaps the technology will exist one day to transport this "advice from the future" back into my more youthful hands. Even if that never happens, at least this will be here for my kids to see, and for you to see too. Go to patflynn.com/letgo-videos/#bonuschapter to watch my "Advice to My Younger Self" video.

Part 2

Here's the video of me interviewing Keoni:
smartpassiveincome.com/letgo-keoni

For the opener to my keynote speech at the 2015 NMX conference, I recreated a scene from my favorite movie, *Back to the Future*—with a real DeLorean in it. Watch it here:
smartpassiveincome.com/letgonmxbonus

Here's the full version of Will Smith's skydiving speech that I referenced in the "Let Go and Let In" chapter:
smartpassiveincome.com/letgowillsmithbonus

PAT'S BOOK CLUB

Thank you again for reading this 10-Year Anniversary Edition of *Let Go*! If it resonated with you, then I'd love to welcome you into my special book club.

The SPI Book Club is a community of passionate readers seeking stories that will stick in their brains and inspire their lives long after they've read them. Sound like a place for you? Subscribe to the SPI Book Club for free and enjoy a featured book recommendation each month, possibly with some exclusive deals to boot!

To join, just go to smartpassiveincome.com/book-club. It's free forever, and a fun way to help each other let go.

I appreciate you! Cheers!

RESOURCES

Over the past decade, I've built and curated a huge trove of resources to help you in your entrepreneurial journey. I've listed them all here for easy reference.

Learn Directly from Pat

From the blog that started it all, to the popular *Smart Passive Income* and *AskPat* podcasts, to ebooks, online courses, and webinars, here is the wealth of resources I've created, much of it available for free, to guide you and inspire you on your journey.

Blog

The Smart Passive Income blog (smartpassiveincome.com/blog) is where it all started, and I still keep it updated with great content, including articles, podcast episodes, income reports, success stories from others, and podcast episodes.

Books

Let Go (Original Edition): smartpassiveincome.com/letgofirstedamazon
Will It Fly?: smartpassiveincome.com/will-it-fly

Ebooks

Ebooks the Smart Way:
smartpassiveincome.com/ebooks-the-smart-way
Email the Smart Way: smartpassiveincome.com/email-the-smart-way
Affiliate Marketing the Smart Way: smartpassiveincome.com/affiliate-marketing-smart-way/

Courses

Smart from Scratch:
courses.smartpassiveincome.com/p/smart-from-scratch
Will It Fly? Companion Course:
courses.smartpassiveincome.com/p/willitfly
Power-Up Podcasting: PowerUpPodcasting.com
Build Your Own Brand: smartpassiveincome.com/byob

Podcasts and Webinars

The SPI Podcast: smartpassiveincome.com/podcasts
The AskPat Podcast: smartpassiveincome.com/ask-pat
SPI TV: smartpassiveincome.com/tv
1 Day Business Breakthrough: 1DayBB.com
SPI Live: smartpassiveincome.com/live

Other Trusted Resources

In addition to the resources I've created myself, I maintain a curated list of the tools, books, websites, and other resources I strongly recommend for building and optimizing your business, right on my website.

Go to smartpassiveincome.com/resources and click on Entrepreneurial Journey to check them out.

Giving Back

As you learned in the book, Pencils of Promise (PencilsofPromise.org) is an organization that's close to my heart for the great work they do building schools in underserved areas.

ACKNOWLEDGMENTS & CREDITS

Let Go is my story, but it would have never happened without some very special people in my life.

To my mom, thank you for showing me the joy that can come with serving others. To my dad, thank you for raising me to always keep my head up and look toward the future. To my wife, April, words cannot express how thankful I am for you. I'm truly blessed to have an amazing wife and super mom like you in my life—I love you so much. To my son, Keoni, and my daughter, Kailani, thank you for being my daily source of inspiration and why I'm so excited to wake up every single morning.

To the entire *Let Go* team, this project is as much yours as it is mine. To Matt, thank you for coming on as a producer, keeping things organized, and creating something more amazing than I could have ever done on my own. To Caleb, your talents never cease to impress me. Thank you for bringing the text in the first edition of my book to life through film. Thank you as well to the rest of the team that helped make this book a reality, including Ray Sylvester, Karen Beattie, Phil Franks, Janna Maron, and Elise LeBreton.

Thank you to Jeremy and Jason from *Internet Business Mastery* for your podcast, inspiration, and guidance when I needed it. Also, thanks to all of the friends and colleagues that have influenced me in one way or another over the years.

To all of the Smart Passive Income fans, I love you all. I hope to continue to pay you back for all of your generosity and support.

And finally, thank you to my previous employer for letting me go, and letting me fly.

ABOUT PAT FLYNN

Pat Flynn is a beloved thought leader in the areas of online entrepreneurship, digital marketing, and lifestyle businesses. He overcame career adversity at an early age by finding his own path and true passion. Despite his success in business, Pat's greatest joys are spending time with his family and friends as well as helping inspire and educate others on how to succeed with their own entrepreneurial careers.

Since 2014, however, he's become more interested in areas of philanthropy, specifically in the world of education. He is on the advisory board for Pencils of Promise, and has helped build schools in Ghana, Africa. He plans to use his success to help education locally, a passion of his now especially since his two young children are now of school age.

Pat is routinely praised for his authentic leadership style and business principles. *Forbes* recently named him one of the ten most transparent leaders in business. The *New York Times* has profiled him as a case study in smart online business building. And countless podcasts and blogs have featured his story and the techniques he uses to manage and grow his audience.

Pat enjoys focusing on writing books, growing his top-ranked business podcast, and speaking at conferences, and learning more about changing education and how kids learn.

To learn more about Pat and what makes him tick, visit patflynn.com.

TO YOU, MY FRIEND,

If you're reading this letter, that means you and I have spent some time together here in this book. I'm incredibly thankful for that, and I hope my story and the lessons I've shared with you have inspired you in some way.

Before you go, I want to challenge you.

This may be out of your comfort zone, but hopefully by now you understand how rewarding it can be to step outside of that zone. And don't worry, you won't have to share what I'm about to ask you to do with anyone else.

Inside the back cover of this book, you may have already noticed a pocket that includes a blank piece of paper and an envelope.

On the envelope, you'll notice a blank line. On that line, write down the date exactly one year from today. So if today is June 17, 2018, write down June 17, 2019, on the envelope.

On the piece of paper, I want you to write a letter to yourself one year from now, sharing all of the things you're going to let go of between now and then—all that you know is holding you back from where you know you want to be.

Think of it as a promise to your future self. What do you promise to let go of?

Fold and place the letter inside the envelope, seal it, and before you put it somewhere safe, snap a photo of the sealed envelope and write me a quick note on your favorite social media platform, using the hashtag #MyPromisetoLetGo, so I can track it.

Put a reminder in your calendar a year from now to open up your letter, and then place the letter somewhere safe.

Here's to you and your future. Thank you for making *Let Go* and my story a part of it.

Cheers!

Flynnspired Productions
An imprint of Flynndustries, LLC
www.smartpassiveincome.com

ISBN 978-0-9970823-4-0 (hbk.)
ISBN 978-0-9970823-2-6 (ebook)

Produced by Page Two
www.pagetwostrategies.com
Cover and interior design by Peter Cocking
Illustrations by Michelle Clement
Edited by Winning Edits · www.winningedits.com
Proofread by Alison Strobel
Printed and bound in Canada by Friesens

18 19 20 21 22 23   5 4 3 2 1

———

Learn more on the website: www.patflynn.com/letgo

———